THE INTERNAL MOTHER

THE INTERNAL MOTHER
Conceptual and Technical Aspects of Object Constancy

edited by
SALMAN AKHTAR, M.D.
SELMA KRAMER, M.D.
and **HENRI PARENS**, M.D.

JASON ARONSON INC.
Northvale, New Jersey
London

This book was set in 12 point Bem by TechType of Upper Saddle River, New Jersey, and printed and bound by Book-mart Press of North Bergen, New Jersey.

Library of Congress Cataloging-in-Publication Data

The internal mother : conceptual and technical aspects of object
    constancy / edited by Salman Akhtar, Selma Kramer, and Henri Parens.
        p.   cm.
    Papers originally presented at the second International Margaret
S. Mahler Symposium on Child Development held on July 31, 1993, in
Cologne, Germany.
    Includes bibliographical references and index.
    ISBN 1-56821-651-3 (alk. paper)
    1. Object constancy (Psychoanalysis)—Congresses.   I. Akhtar,
Salman, 1946 July 31–   II. Kramer, Selma.   III. Parens, Henri, 1928–
    IV. International Margaret S. Mahler Symposium on Child
Development (2nd : 1993 : Cologne, Germany)
BF175.5.O22I57   1996
150.19′5—dc20   94-31219

Manufactured in the United States of America. Jason Aronson Inc. offers books and cassettes. For information and catalog write to Jason Aronson Inc., 230 Livingston Street, Northvale, New Jersey 07647.

To the memory

of

Margaret S. Mahler,

teacher, friend, source of inspiration

Contents

4

The Development of Object Constancy
and Its Deviations   93
Phyllis Tyson, PH.D.

5

Winnicott's Notion of the Use of an Object   115
Discussion of Phyllis Tyson's Chapter
"The Development of Object Constancy
and Its Deviations"
Lore Schacht, M.D.

6

Object Constancy and
Adult Psychopathology   127
Salman Akhtar, M.D.

7

Problems in the Developmental
Conceptualization of Adult Psychopathology
and Its Treatment   157
Discussion of Akhtar's Chapter "Object Constancy
and Adult Psychopathology"
Ludwig Haesler, M.D.

8

Perspectives on Internalization,
Consolidation, and Change   173
Concluding Reflections
Harold P. Blum, M.D.

Acknowledgment

The chapters in this book were originally presented at the Second International Margaret S. Mahler Symposium on Child Development held on July 31, 1993, in Cologne, Germany. Since this was truly an international effort, sponsors and colleagues from both sides of the Atlantic deserve our gratitude.

On the European side, the first person we wish to acknowledge is Dr. Lotte Koehler of Munich, Germany, who was most generous in her help and sponsorship of the symposium. We are thankful to the four German psychoanalysts who participated in the program and whose contributions appear in this book. They are Drs. Eva Berberich, Ludwig Haesler, Paul Janssen, and Lore Schacht. We also wish to acknowledge the European leaders and co-leaders of the workshops that followed the symposium, namely, Drs. Ernest Abelin, Rainer Krause, Johannes Lehtonen, and Bettina Meissner. We also received help from the René A. Spitz-Gesellschaft, from Prof. Dr. med. K. Koehle and his indefatigable assistant Dr. G. Happenkamps (both of the Institute and Policlinic for Psychosomatic Medicine and Psychotherapy at the University of Cologne), as well as from Prof. F.v. Boxberg of the Psychoanalytic Arbeitsgemeinschaft Köln-Düsseldorf.

On the American side, we wish to express our deepest gratitude to the Margaret S. Mahler Psychiatric Research Foundation for its sponsorship of the symposium. We are profoundly indebted to Dr. Herman Staples (whose recent and untimely death we regret and mourn) and his wife, Mary Staples, for their skillful and devoted help in organizing this international event. Many other American colleagues, especially Drs. Harold Blum, LeRoy Byerly, and Donald Meyers, devoted time and energy to conceptualizing and organizing the symposium, and we express our gratitude to them. Many others, including Drs. Patricia Nachman, Lilo Plaschkes, and Vamik Volkan, participated in the symposium as workshop leaders, and we acknowledge this valuable collaboration here. We are also grateful to Dr. Troy L. Thompson II, Chairman, Department of Psychiatry and Human Behavior, Jefferson Medical College, as well as to many colleagues in the Philadelphia Psychoanalytic Institute and Society for their moral and intellectual support during the symposium and the publication of its proceedings. Ms. Gloria Schwartz provided skillful secretarial assistance for the organization of the symposium, and Ms. Maryann Nevin for the preparation of this book's manuscript. We thank them both here.

Contributors

Salman Akhtar, M.D.
Professor of Psychiatry, Jefferson Medical College; Training and Supervising Analyst, Philadelphia Psychoanalytic Institute, Philadelphia, Pennsylvania

Eva Berberich, M.D.
Training and Supervising Analyst, Psychoanalytic Institute, Heidelberg, Germany

Anni Bergman, Ph.D.
Faculty, Clinical Psychology Doctoral Program, City University of New York; Member, Society for Freudian Psychologists, New York

Harold P. Blum, M.D.
Clinical Professor of Psychiatry, New York University Medical College; Training and Supervising Analyst, The Psychoanalytic Institute, New York University Medical Center; Executive Director, Sigmund Freud Archives, New York

Ludwig Haesler, M.D.
Training and Supervising Analyst, Sigmund Freud Institute Frankfurt/Main; Visiting Lecturer of Psychotherapy and Psychoanalysis, Friedrich-Schiller University, Jena, Germany

Paul L. Janssen, M.D.
Professor, Department of Psychosomatic Medicine and Psychotherapy, Ruhr-University, Bochum, Germany

Selma Kramer, M.D.
Professor of Psychiatry, Jefferson Medical College; Training and Supervising Analyst, Philadelphia Psychoanalytic Institute, Philadelphia, Pennsylvania

John B. McDevitt, M.D.
Training and Supervising Analyst, New York University Psychoanalytic Institute; Director of Research, Margaret S. Mahler Psychiatric Research Foundation, New York

Helen C. Meyers, M.D.
Clinical Professor of Psychiatry, College of Physicians and Surgeons, Columbia University; Training and Supervising Analyst, Columbia University Center for Psychoanalytic Training and Research, New York

Henri Parens, M.D.
Professor of Psychiatry, Jefferson Medical College; Training and Supervising Analyst, Philadelphia Psychoanalytic Institute, Philadelphia, Pennsylvania

Lore Schacht, M.D.
Training and Supervising Analyst, Child Analyst, Psychoanalytic Institute, Freiburg, Germany

Phyllis Tyson, Ph.D.
Associate Clinical Professor of Psychiatry, University of California, San Diego; Training and Supervising Analyst, San Diego Psychoanalytic Society, California

1

MULTIPLE PERSPECTIVES ON OBJECT CONSTANCY

Selma Kramer, M.D.
and Henri Parens, M.D.

Object constancy denotes and explains a phenomenon of vital importance to healthy psychic development, adaptation, and object relations. Not, according to Mahler, merely an endpoint of the separation–individuation process, object constancy is an acquired capability that requires a stable "structuring of the libidinal object" (Spitz 1946, 1954, 1965), the stable evolving of "attachment" to the object (Bowlby 1958), the securing of "basic trust" and a "sense of autonomy" (Erikson 1959). Most commonly, it requires the implementation of that remarkable phenomenon, the transitional object (Winnicott 1953 [1951]), and eventually the child's achieving the ability to "use the object" (Winnicott 1968) as the child progresses from symbiotic oneness (Mahler 1965, Mahler et al. 1975) with the structuring libidinal object to separateness from that now internally stable libidinal object in object constancy.

THE CONCEPT OF OBJECT CONSTANCY

Hartmann introduced the concept object constancy in 1952 [1951]; it is one of his several major contributions to classical object relations theory. In Chapter 2 of this volume, John McDevitt details the historical development of the concept, including the debate that followed from the different defining achievements given to the concept by A. Freud (1963, 1965) and Spitz (1965), and by Hartmann (1952) and Mahler (1965). In addition to anchoring the capability for object constancy to the point at which the infant can maintain the cathexis of the object, whether the object satisfies or frustrates, we agree with Spitz that the sufficient structuring of the libidinal object is a key factor in the object's acquiring "constancy." This is an important achievement in the infant, an achievement that has some degree of stability, since separation anxiety, stranger anxiety, and reunion reactions give clear evidence of the infant's having achieved the ability for recognitive memory—which requires that an internal representation exist even though it is retrievable only under specific conditions, namely, the actual visualization of the object externally (see also Fraiberg 1969). Prior to the felicitous introduction of Piaget's work into analytic thought (Anthony 1956, Wolff 1960), Spitz (1946, 1954) had already described and conceptualized well the progressive structuring of the libidinal object even without the added understanding of the evolving of memory developed, independently of course, by Piaget (1954).

As McDevitt points out, Hartmann's original definition required achievements of ego functioning assumed by psychoanalytic infant observers to be not yet attained at 6 to 8 months, that is, the age of the structuring of the libidinal object. These achievements include the ability to retain positive cathexis of the object in the face of hostile destructive wishes toward it, and the management of ambivalence, that is, the ego's ability to maintain the positive cathexis of the object while under duress created by the intraagency conflict between love and hate feelings toward that object. Even assumptions of the earliest experiences of ambivalence occurring from the end of the first year of life (Abraham 1924, Parens 1979) do not assume the ego's sufficient mastery of ambivalence to preserve object cathexis without evoking splitting or other representational antiintegrating defenses. McDevitt makes much sense to us in proposing that the further evolution of ambivalence during the rapprochement crisis must come under sufficient ego control for hate not to be experienced by the ego as threatening to good object representation (cathexis) (see also Burgner and Edgcumbe 1972). Conceptually, this fits the definition originally proposed by Hartmann. Thus, the argument that although we must recognize that the structuring of the libidinal object (as well as "attachment" as similarly conceptualized by Bowlby [1958]), and Anna Freud's (1965) nodal shift from inability to ability to maintain the cathexis of the object whether it gratifies or frustrates, all suggest a level of stability of internalized object relatedness that does not reflect the substantially greater level of structuring, stabilization, and psychic accessibility that comes with the attainment of libidinal object constancy as conceptualized by Mahler.

Another important issue pertains to the question of object constancy. It is readily solvable and may, indeed, already have been solved. Years ago Parens (1972) expressed concern that the assumption that object constancy means that there is stability and accessibility to positively cathected internal objects might mislead us to assume that there is no "constancy" (meaning stability and accessibility) to hostile and hateful internalized objects or introjects. Clinical experience with borderline and psychotic (Ekstein 1971) children and adults very much teaches us otherwise, as the literature on borderline disorders and their treatment amply documents. In addition, the resistance to change of such introjects is only too well known to all depth psychology clinicians, suggesting a remarkable degree of stability, and not just accessibility but pervasiveness. Blum (1981) may have solved the problem for us by proposing the concept of object inconstancy. Whatever solution we adopt, we find it useful to identify this problem in the theory.

We should also note that Mahler (1965) wisely availed herself of Piaget's concept of object permanence and therewith of evocative memory (also Mahler et al. 1975); however, as McDevitt (1975) has pointed out, and points out again in this volume, these are obligatory but insufficient capabilities for the attainment of libidinal object constancy. Whereas the former are cognitive developmental milestones that are built in to become functional at around 14 to 18 months of age, object constancy requires good-enough object relational experiences for its structuralization. This was already emphasized by Spitz's concept the *libidinal* object.

The concept, as used by Hartmann as well as by Mahler and McDevitt, means that the internal object, now separated in the child's mind from individuated self-representations, stands stably as an internal structure to which the child (self) can turn in times of need—and even when not needed—as the latency-age child who can go out and play with an inner sense of security and relatedness, knowing that Mother is in the house or readily accessible intrapsychically if and when needed. We note that this line of thinking highlights a sharp distinction between Mahler (ego psychological object relations theory) and Kohut (self psychology): Is there a place in self psychology for the concept of object constancy given that all internalizations are construed to be "selfobjects"?

One more point: Like Kernberg (1967, 1975) and Mahler (1971), we have found that splitting results from the ego's intolerance of ambivalence toward the libidinal object. Kernberg has, of course, made this the hallmark of borderline functioning and character formation. We have also found, however, along lines raised by Helen Meyers in this volume, that some degree of splitting occurs among neurotic patients as well, but does not enduringly erode object constancy in these patients. Like Frank (1992), we have found areas of weakness or of vulnerability in object constancy in especially traumatized neurotics who, for example, find separation from the transference object extremely painful.

MULTIPLE PERSPECTIVES

Now to the contents of this book. John B. McDevitt, one of Mahler's principal collaborators, begins Chapter 2 by reviewing the history of the concept of object constancy, providing a sequel and update to the survey of its evolution in analytic theory written by Selma Fraiberg in 1969.

As is typical in his writings, McDevitt illustrates his findings from direct observations with children and the analysis of an adult, and makes the point that "the most common references to disturbances in object constancy in the literature are in the context of borderline patients." McDevitt goes beyond his 1975 description of the evolution of object constancy during the first two years, detailing its development during the third year and after. He makes a number of important points, among them that object constancy is not absolute: "it may be useful to think of degrees of attainment of object constancy"; and that "object constancy does not become a component of . . . conflict as does the superego."

In her discussion of McDevitt's paper (Chapter 3), Eva Berberich points out that the application of Mahler and McDevitt's concept of libidinal object constancy to more serious pathologies is not used in Germany to the degree that it is in the United States. The concept of "lack of object constancy, or disturbed object constancy," while taught in German analytic institutes, is not readily implemented in clinical work with more disturbed patients.

Berberich describes her work with a mother and 10-month-old child dyad in a conjoint treatment, a model developed by Mahler (her tripartite model) and continued by Anni Bergman and Eleanor Galenson. Our experiences in such cases support Berberich, who draws attention to the changes effected in the mother (parents) by the conjoint treatment and the dramatic changes it can bring about in both child and parent. Berberich's report of her treatment of Lili and her mother adds to reports by others of such work (including not only Mahler, and Bergman and Galenson, but also Fraiberg and a number of her collaborators, as well as Sally Provence and others).

Anni Bergman also collaborated with Mahler and is currently a collaborator with McDevitt in their follow-up study of the children originally studied by the central Margaret S. Mahler Research Project. In Chapter 4 she elaborates on "the fourth subphase . . . on the way to object constancy," drawing comparisons between the attainment of object constancy in separation-individuation theory and the working through of the depressive position of Kleinian theory.

Bergman raises important questions about McDevitt's cases. Citing examples from her own work, for instance, she wonders how McDevitt's Donna dealt with her experiences of her mother as the bad mother, that is, the mother who leaves her. She calls for further exploration of some of McDevitt's speculations about how boys and girls resolve their rapprochement crises. Bergman then also presents a study of a boy passing through his separation-individuation into object constancy whom she later saw as an adult in follow-up, as well as the case of a child who suffered from her mother's being insufficiently emotionally available to her.

Paul L. Janssen adds to McDevitt's thesis of the usefulness of the concept of object constancy for clinical work by presenting in Chapter 5 a case from the psychosomatic unit where he and his colleagues work. In the course of detailing the reconstructive inferences he and his colleagues came to regarding the patient, Janssen hypothesizes: "The irreconcilable split between [her] body and soul . . . was in fact a consequence of the medicalized and instrumentalized handling her body had received in her initial phase of life. She had become fixated on the instrumental mother (the incubator)." We draw attention to this hypothesis because it has become an area of inquiry of much interest to some of our colleagues. To be sure, the patient's mother's implied difficulties in Janssen's brief description of her compel us to assume a substantial disturbance in her and emotional unavailability to her infant. Furthermore, our colleague Barbara Shapiro, a practicing pediatrician and psychoanalytic candidate, believes the pain induced by the instrumentalizations to which many premature infants are subjected may play a key part in their evolving character formation. It is clearly an area requiring exploration from the psychoanalytic vantage point.

Janssen discusses "cognitive defects," that is, structural ego defects of memory retrieval and problems these may produce in analytic psychotherapy. And he also introduces us to a physical contact, "concentrative movement therapy," a "body therapy" that he tells us is in much use in Germany with significantly disturbed patients.

In Chapter 6 Helen Meyers goes beyond McDevitt's proposing that there are degrees of attainment of object constancy. She asks whether the development of object constancy goes on throughout life, whether the object can be partially constant or must be all or nothing, and whether, once established, it fluctuates. "Is it subject to regression, splitting, and disintegration," she asks, "[even] in ordinary neurotics under stress?" And, "Does the establishment of object constancy have to include the *working through* of ambivalence . . . or does it involve the *tolerance* of ambivalence?" To Meyers's "way of thinking, object constancy is really more of a *capacity* to maintain constant objects, than a specific object relationship—and this capacity . . . , once established, . . . does not get lost."

The next section of the book, Chapters 7 and 8, constitutes a major presentation by Phyllis Tyson, followed by a discussion by Lore Schacht.

Phyllis Tyson further details for us the vicissitudes of the concept of object constancy. She proposes a way to bring together the differing conceptualizations of each of the major theorists, Hartmann, Spitz, Anna Freud, Piaget, and Mahler, and in the course of doing so, raises some questions and proposes some interesting ideas of her own. Looking at a specific aspect of object constancy, namely, its ego-functioning parameter, Tyson introduces Winnicott's concept of the use of the object into the further exploration of object constancy, and the means implemented by the young child in attaining it.

Tyson poses an interesting challenge to the reader in her exercise of seeing the child's use of the mother in the child's modes of coping with and regulating affects, and asks whether the issue should be one of "inadequate mother, or inadequate baby?" Tyson's proposing the ego function that can use affects as signals in the service of self-regulation may be a conceptualization that has long awaited further examination and definition, perhaps, in fact, since Freud proposed the signal theory of anxiety in 1926.

In Chapter 8, Lore Schacht traces some of the steps taken by Hartmann in conceptualizing object constancy and by Winnicott in conceiving the "use" of the object, and elaborates a difference in understanding of Winnicott's concept between herself and Tyson. Schacht notes that the concept of the transitional object seems to not have received sufficient acknowledgement for its "integrative function" on the way to object constancy. Those of us who had the good fortune to be among Mahler's students know that the idea of the transitional object, as well as the "structuring of the libidinal object" (Spitz 1965), insufficiently written about these days, were used by Mahler in her everyday thinking and work. These major concepts were part of the foundation on which Mahler and her collaborators constructed the notion of separation–individuation. Mahler was committed to, and focused on, testing and elaborating her model of this specific development, as McDevitt and Bergman confirm in this volume. It is perhaps more up to those among us who for one reason or another attempt to pull together the major contributions of developmental psychoanalysis to integrate the critical role played by the transitional object in the development toward object constancy (e.g., Parens 1991).

Chapters 9 and 10 comprise a presentation by Salman Akhtar and discussion by Ludwig Haesler. Akhtar looks at the applicability and usefulness of the development of object constancy in analytic therapy of adults. Known for his analytic clinical and theoretical work with borderline and narcissistically disordered patients, Akhtar focuses especially on the contributions made by Mahler in refining the concept of libidinal object constancy. He discusses "the challenges to object constancy" posed by development, especially the Oedipus complex, latency, adolescence, young adulthood, and middle age. The greatest period of challenge to object constancy may be late adulthood. Erikson (1959) treated the issue of ego identity beautifully with regard to its functions and challenges during late adulthood. A complementary exploration of the contributions of object constancy to and the challenges posed to it by late adulthood would further enrich our understanding of and clinical work with the elderly. But the reader who wishes to pursue this question on his or her own will find the task facilitated by following Akhtar's model for such an exploration.

Following this exploration, Akhtar presents substantial clinical material from which he discerns pathological syn-

dromes that he believes arise from failures to achieve sufficiently adequate and stable object constancy. He concludes his
presentation by looking at some implications of these concepts for the clinical psychoanalytic process and for technique.

In his discussion of Akhtar's presentation, Ludwig
Haesler asks whether we can apply "a theoretical concept like
object constancy in the manner of a medical diagnosis."
Haesler cautions us against idealizing one model of development, indeed, just one aspect of development, separation-
individuation theory, over other component theories, each of
which gives us a working construct that guides us in understanding but a part of the complex fabric that constitutes each
person.

In the final chapter Harold Blum places the development
of the concept of object constancy not just along the path of
the evolution of the concept itself but in a general historical
frame of psychoanalytic thought from Freud on. He then
retraces the content of the volume with brief discussions of
each contributor's essay. He closes with a call for well-
reasoned progress in our field.

CONCLUSION

The editors of this volume and the colleagues who made the
symposium so successful hope that our German, indeed, our
European colleagues will find these pages useful. Given Berberich's observation that separation-individuation theory is
not much used clinically in Germany, it may be so as well for
the rest of Europe. We would be gratified were this volume to
arouse further interest than now exists among our European
colleagues in the enormously valuable additional guide that
separation-individuation theory, and object constancy specifically, provides in our clinical work. The editors are persuaded
that psychoanalytic understanding of our patients can be

further enhanced by the addition of this model of development and adaptation to the collective chest of theories, metapsychological and clinical, that constitute psychoanalysis.

REFERENCES

Abraham, K. (1924). A short study of the development of libido. In *Selected Papers of Karl Abraham*, pp. 418–501. New York: Basic Books, 1953.

Anthony, E. J. (1956). Six applications de la théorie génétique de Piaget à la théorie et à la pratique psycho-dynamique. *Revue Suisse de Psychologie Pure et Appliquée* 15.

Blum, H. P. (1981). Object inconstancy and paranoid conspiracy. *Journal of the American Psychoanalytic Association* 29:789–813.

Bowlby, J. A. (1958). The nature of the child's tie to his mother. *International Journal of Psycho-Analysis* 39:350–373.

Burgner, M., and Edgcumbe, R. (1972). Some problems in the conceptualization of early object relations. Part 2. The concept of object constancy. *Psychoanalytic Study of the Child* 27:315–333. New York: Quadrangle Books.

Ekstein, R. (1971). *The Challenge: Despair and Hope in the Conquest of Inner Space*. New York: Brunner/Mazel.

Erikson, E. H. (1959). *Identity and the Life Cycle. Psychological Issues*, Monograph 1. New York: International Universities Press.

Fraiberg, S. (1969). Libidinal object constancy and mental representation. *Psychoanalytic Study of the Child* 24:9–47. New York: International Universities Press.

Frank, A. (1992). A problem with the couch: incapacities and conflicts. In *When the Body Speaks*, ed. S. Kramer and S. Akhtar, pp. 90–112. Northvale, NJ: Jason Aronson.

Freud, A. (1963). The concept of developmental lines. *Psychoanalytic Study of the Child* 18:245–265. New York: International Universities Press.

———— (1965). *Normality and Pathology in Childhood: Assessments of Development*. New York: International Universities Press.

Hartmann, H. (1952). The mutual influences in the development of the ego and the id. In *Essays on Ego Psychology*, pp. 155–181. New York: International Universities Press, 1964.

Kernberg, O. F. (1967). Borderline personality organization. *Journal of the American Psychoanalytic Association* 15:641–685.

———— (1975). *Borderline Conditions and Pathological Narcissism*. New York: Jason Aronson.

Mahler, M. S. (1965). On the significance of the normal separation–individuation phase. In *Drives, Affects, Behavior*, vol. 2, ed. M. Schur, pp. 161–169. New York: International Universities Press.

———— (1971). A study of the separation–individuation process and its possible application to borderline phenomena in the psychoanalytic situation. *Psychoanalytic Study of the Child* 26:403–424. New Haven: Yale University Press.

Mahler, M. S., Pine, F., and Bergman, A. (1975). *The Psychological Birth of the Human Infant.* New York: Basic Books.

McDevitt, J. B. (1975). Separation-individuation and object constancy. *Journal of the American Psychoanalytic Association* 23:713–742.

Parens, H. (1972). Book review: Rudolph Ekstein's *The Challenge: Despair and Hope in the Conquest of Inner Space. Psychoanalytic Quarterly* 41:616–623.

———— (1979). *The Development of Aggression in Early Childhood.* New York: Jason Aronson.

———— (1991). Separation-individuation theory and psychosexual theory. In *Beyond the Symbiotic Orbit: Advances in Separation-Individuation Theory. Essays in Honor of Selma Kramer, M.D.*, ed. S. Akhtar and H. Parens, pp. 3–34. Hillsdale, NJ: Analytic Press.

Piaget, J. (1954). *Les Relations entre l'affectivité et l'intélligence dans le développement mental de l'enfant.* Paris: Centre de Documentation Universitaire.

Spitz, R. A. (1946). The smiling response: a contribution to the ontogenesis of social relations. *Genetic Psychology Monographs* 34:57–125.

———— (1954). Genèse des premières relations objectales. *Revue Française de Psycho-Analyse* 28.

———— (1965). *The First Year of Life.* New York: International Universities Press.

Winnicott, D. W. (1953). Transitional objects and transitional phenomena: a study of the first not-me possession. *International Journal of Psycho-Analysis* 34:89–97.

———— (1968). The use of an object and relating through identifications. In *Playing and Reality,* pp. 86–94. London: Tavistock, 1971.

Wolff, P. H. (1960). *The Developmental Psychologies of Jean Piaget and Psychoanalysis. Psychological Issues,* Monograph 5. New York: International Universities Press.

2

THE CONCEPT OF OBJECT CONSTANCY AND ITS CLINICAL APPLICATIONS

John B. McDevitt, M.D.

The term *object constancy* was introduced by Hartmann in 1952 in an object relations context. Achieving object constancy has since been generally accepted as an important stage in the development of object relations. Also generally accepted is that this achievement refers to both libidinal and cognitive aspects of the child's attachment to the mother. There has been less agreement among psychoanalysts, however, regarding the definition of object constancy, when it is usually achieved, the criteria for evaluating whether or not it has been achieved, and its clinical use. These are considerations I address in what follows.

THE CONCEPTUAL BACKDROP

Both Anna Freud (1965) and Spitz (Spitz and Cobliner 1965) refer to the 8-month-old infant's libidinal attachment to the mother as the beginning of the attainment of object constancy. Anna Freud (Panel 1968) wrote,

> What we mean by object constancy is the child's capacity to keep up object cathexis irrespective of frustration or satisfaction. At the time before object constancy the child withdraws cathexis from the unsatisfactory or unsatisfying object—the turning toward the object takes place again when the wish or need arises. After object constancy has been established the person representing the object keeps this place for the child whether he satisfies or frustrates. [1968, p. 506]

Her use of the term *constancy* connotes stability of object cathexis.

Fraiberg (1969) adds to this the requirement of having acquired object permanence in the cognitive realm of development, employing Piaget's (1937) criteria for the emergence of evocative memory at 18 months. This memory, unlike recognition memory, has relative autonomy from the stimuli of exteroceptive experience and the stimulus of drives and need states.

Mahler (1965) places the attainment of object constancy later, using, in addition to the criteria of the libidinal bond and evocative memory, the criterion of the child's ability to tolerate brief physical separations from the mother. In her view the conflicts and ambivalence present during the rapprochement subphase must be resolved before we can speak of the attainment of some measure of object constancy. For this to occur, the "good" and "bad" objects must be unified in a single representation, which customarily takes place in the third year. This enables aggressive and libidinal drives to fuse, tempers hostility, and fosters the predominance of the defense mechanism of repression over that of splitting (Mahler et al. 1975). Mahler (1968) wrote, "By object constancy we mean that the maternal image has become intrapsychically available to the child in the same way as the actual mother had been libidinally available—for sustenance, comfort, and love" (p. 222).

Sandler and Joffe (1966, p. 343) wrote that "the component which differentiates constant object relationships from need-satisfying ones is a contribution of the ego, an additional affective ego value cathexis which we could describe in terms such as 'nonsensual love,' 'esteem for the object,' etc. This is not the same as the aim-inhibited instinctual components." Affective value cathexis refers to an enduring nonsensual affective attachment that persists independent of need satisfaction.

Burgner and Edgcumbe (1972), like Anna Freud, consider the establishment of object constancy to mark the transition from the need-satisfying type of relationship to more mature psychological object relationships. Developmentally, its attainment denotes the individual's capacity to differentiate between objects and to maintain a relationship to one specific object regardless of whether needs are being satisfied or not. They add that the capacity for complete relationships is a progression that also involves tolerance of opposing affects of love and hate and an affective relationship with the love object. They consider the acquisition of the "capacity for constant relationships" to be a "crucial switch point" in the development of object relations that requires the maturation and development of several capacities in the areas of drives, ego, and affects. If this capacity for constant relationships is not established, subsequent development in all areas will be severely distorted.

I have elsewhere (McDevitt 1975) described the steps leading to the attainment of object constancy. Each step is marked by a new level of selfobject differentiation and a new level of self and object stability. Prior to the acquisition of each new level, there are transitional periods of psychic disequilibrium evidenced by anxiety that is appropriate to the danger situation that exists at the time. Only slowly is each period of disequilibrium resolved by the acquisition of new faculties leading to the establishment of a more differentiated and more stable mental representation of the mother and of the self. From 6 to 14 months, during the differentiation and practicing subphases of the separation–individuation process, the infant must learn to cope with and to tolerate stranger anxiety and the anxiety aroused by physical separation from the mother, by the fear of object loss.

Soon after he or she has made progress in that direction during the practicing subphase, the toddler is confronted with the task of coping with the painful feelings of separateness and aloneness brought on by the obligatory process of intrapsychic separation in the rapprochement subphase. In addition to the fear of object loss, he or she now fears the loss of the object's love. Following this is the need to resolve the ambivalence and conflicts that exist in relationship with the mother during the rapprochement crisis, partly by means of identification. This new period of disequilibrium is not resolved until well into the third year, at which time the child may be confronted once again with another period of disequilibrium brought on by conflicts associated with castration anxiety.

I also wrote,

> The ability to tolerate separation from the mother during the third year of life indicates that although the specific libidinal attachment to the mother, along with progress in the invariant, largely autonomous sequences in cognitive development are *necessary* conditions for the gradual attainment of object constancy, they are not *sufficient* conditions for it; the *essential* determinants are the nature of the cathexis of the mental representation of the mother and what might be called the quality of this representation. [p. 733]

I would add now, adopting Burgner and Edgcumbe's terms, that each of the steps I have described contain switch points.

A wide range of disturbances in object constancy have been reported in the psychoanalytic literature. Let me review briefly a few of these. The most severe disturbances in object constancy are seen in children who have suffered repeated or prolonged periods of deprivation, for example, children reared in institutions or in multiple foster home placements (Solnit 1982). In these children language and thought may be delayed, and the emotional ties to people are shallow and promiscuous, severely limiting the formation of identifications. They immediately search for new objects when frustrated. They have little capacity for intimacy, tenderness, or empathy. The analysis of a concentration camp victim (Gyomroi 1963) showed that the patient's object relations were so primitive that she longed more for need satisfaction than she longed for the need-satisfying object.

Edgcumbe and Burgner (1972, Burgner and Edgcumbe 1972) examined the clinical material in the Hampstead Index. They wrote,

> We would suggest that, strictly speaking, later relationships should be characterized as need-satisfying only if the early mode of relating to the object belonging to the stage of need-satisfying relationships persists, or is regressively revived, entirely unchanged; that is to say, if immediate satisfaction of a need is more important than the object that satisfies it. [p. 310]

They compared this with the persistence of other modes of relating to the object early in life such as the persistence of the sadomasochistic relationships appropriate to the toddler in the anal phase.

Total arrest at the need-satisfying stage was found only in some psychotic children whose drive and ego development were also arrested. The only aspect of object constancy present was perceptual (cognitive) constancy. A larger group of severely disturbed neurotic and borderline children at the clinic appeared to relate on a need-satisfying level, although they had progressed to the beginning attainment of object constancy; for example, they expected immediate satisfaction, were unable to tolerate frustration, showed a relative lack of concern for the rights and wishes of others, and lacked interest in aspects of the object other than its capacity to satisfy needs. This defensive regression in object relationships usually centered on fears of destroying or losing the object or the object's love. The aim of the regression was to bind the object more firmly to the child rather than to replace it with substitutes. These children were reluctant to move on to more mature modes of relating and greater independence. Although they appeared to be in the need-satisfying stage, they maintained object cathexis irrespective of satisfaction or frustration.

The most common references to disturbances in object constancy in the literature are in the context of borderline patients.

Kernberg (1975) wrote,

Characteristically, object constancy, or the capacity for establishing 'total' object relationships, is defective in borderline patients, and they express this by their lack of capacity for tolerating ambivalent reactions toward objects. The degree to which borderline patients tolerate simultaneously loving and hateful feelings toward the same person without simply shifting from one extreme set of emotional reactions to an opposite one, is a prognostically favorable indicator of better quality of object relationships. [p. 145]

He agrees with Mahler that these patients had not been able to satisfactorily resolve the conflicts and ambivalence of the rapprochement subphase.

Adler and Buie (1979) offer another point of view. In addition to ambivalence and conflict, they believe that borderline patients have a cognitive defect that explains their painful feelings of "aloneness." They have not achieved solid evocative memory in the area of affective object relationships and are prone to regress to recognition memory or earlier when faced with stress. The most important stress is rage brought on by real or fantasied object loss.

After describing a patient who failed to acquire a stable cognitive achievement of self–other differentiation, a form of pathology stemming from early in the separation-individuation process, Pine (1979) wrote that "patients with defects in the development of libidinal object constancy can be thought of as retaining the basic sense of differentiation but as having difficulty with a next step in the separation-individuation process, that of holding in memory the well-differentiated concept of the other" (p. 235).

To account for certain types of impaired affective and cognitive object constancy, Blum (1981) introduced the concept of *object inconstancy*. Before object constancy is achieved, the caregiver does not have an independent existence and initiative, but is experienced in terms of the child's wishes and boundaries. The inconstant object does not or cannot have time separateness, and the threat of desertion and betrayal is ever present. In some borderlines and in paranoid splitting, the persistent persecutory object is the negative reciprocal of libidinal object constancy. The hated narcissistic object and hated self are linked in incomplete separation–individuation and projective–introjective processes. Because of the desperate need to maintain the inconstant object tie, the paranoid and other borderlines are desperately attached and coercively cling to or are shadowed by the persecutory object. This "attachment" paradoxically attempts to compensate for the comforting, concerned care reliably internalized in object constancy.

Other investigators have described the experience of aloneness in neurotic patients. Frank (1992, also see Fleming

1975) wrote about a neurotic patient who found it difficult to tolerate separations from the analyst or to lie on the couch. In addition to being compromise formations, these difficulties were the result of a defect or incapacity to retain a visual image of the analyst, an incapacity Frank thought began in the rapprochement subphase.

I have elsewhere (McDevitt 1975) traced the development of object constancy during the first two years of life. Here, after briefly recapitulating the events of those first twenty-four months, I elaborate on the events observed during the third year, particularly on the role of identification in the attainment of object constancy.

INSIGHTS FROM CHILD OBSERVATION

Donna

A close, mutually satisfying relation between mother and child was apparent when Donna entered the observational research study of the separation-individuation process at the age of 5 months. Both seemed secure in the relationship, closely attuned to each other, and well matched in temperament. By 6 months, Donna cried briefly when her mother went out of the room for an interview and was restless and unhappy during her absence.

In her eighth month, after her mother left the room, Donna, while mouthing a toy, repeatedly looked at the door without apparent external stimulus and cried bitterly. By this age she had an exclusive attachment to her mother, had a memory of her during her absence, and was aware that her mother's absence caused the distress she experienced. In her ninth month she stayed close to her mother, anxiously anticipating that she might leave the room again.

From 9 to 14 months Donna's cognitive ability to remember her mother when she was out of the room and the cathexis of this memory were too unstable and too fragile to sustain her. One method she, like other infants, used to manage her distress was to regressively withdraw into herself. She looked sad and preoccupied, and lost all interest in her surroundings.

By 14 months Donna had become more independent and self-sufficient. She readily explored and played at some distance from her mother. Although she became quieter and mouthed objects more often during her mother's absences, she was neither sad nor withdrawn and could easily be distracted.

By 18 months when she chose to go to the toddler room without her mother, she would say "Mommy" occasionally but showed neither distress nor the need to seek her mother in the nearby infant room. When asked where her mother was, she pointed in the direction of the infant room.

Donna's sense of well-being was no longer dependent on her mother's presence. It seemed to be maintained instead by a more stable mental representation of the mother. This did not last, however. In her nineteenth month Donna had a mild illness and was given an injection of penicillin. That night she woke and insisted that her father comfort her. When she woke again at 6:30 in the morning, she refused her mother's help and lay against the door to her parents' bedroom, knocking and pleading for her father to come to her.

For the next several months Donna needed to know at all times where her mother was and stayed close to her. At home it was often not sufficient to hear her mother's voice; she had to see her and touch her. At the research nursery she was torn between her need to be with her mother and her wish to play independently, and was uncomfortable doing either. One of the other mothers commented, "There are two things going on at the same time. Donna misses her mother, yet she wants to play."

Whereas formerly Donna had been one of the most assertive and aggressive of the study children, she was no longer able to stand up for herself. She could neither hold on to a toy nor take a toy from another child. She appeared anxious and preoccupied. She was sensitive to criticism, jealous and possessive, and intolerant of frustration.

In contrast to the inhibition of aggression at the research nursery, at home, when she was not clinging to her mother, Donna was imperious, demanding, and coercive. If frustrated or when diapers or clothes needed changing, she fought back or, more often, submitted, screaming and crying.

This crisis in Donna's development during the rapprochement subphase, from 16 to 24 months, occurred more or less in all study children. It was brought on by profound changes in the child's mental and emotional development: the capacity for evocative memory and representational thought, a shift to the anal–sadistic and early genital phases of psychosexual development (Galenson and Roiphe 1971, Roiphe 1968), and a more precise demarcation of the self- and object representation. Because of these changes the child felt small and helpless and realized that her wishes and her mother's did not always coincide.

Thoughts and feelings based on the child's new-found capacity for mental representation of the mother, the self, body parts, particularly the genitals, feelings and wishes, prohibitions, and so forth persisted beyond the situation in which they had their origin. Conflicts with the mother no longer simply flared up and disappeared as they had earlier; they continued in the child's mind for longer periods of time. They were now capable of being held in memory. Conflicts existed between the toddler's wish to get her own way on the one hand and her need to please her mother on the other, between her wish to assert her independence and her dependence on the mother. They also existed internally between the child's wishes and her memory of her mother's expectations and prohibitions.

When aggressive forces outweighed libidinal forces in the junior toddler's mind, her memory of her mother became unstable. It no longer sustained her during her mother's absence as it had a few months earlier. As we have seen, from 8 to 14 months Donna required her mother's presence to be comfortable; from 14 to 18 months she managed well during her mother's absence. From 19 to 25 months she was upset when her mother was absent, and yet not comfortable in her presence because of her ambivalence and conflicts. Her mother could not reassure her or help her resolve her dilemma between clinging and moving away.

In spite of the excellent development of object constancy from 14 to 18 months, Donna's rapprochement crisis was more overtly dramatic than that of most other study children. One reason she was not able to tolerate angry feelings toward her mother was her mother's inability to tolerate her own aggression. The mother was overconcerned, overpermissive, and unable to frustrate Donna. What the mother was neurotically afraid of (her aggression) meant "real" danger to Donna (McDevitt 1991).

From 25 to 29 months Donna was once again able to tolerate her mother's absence better than her peers, as she had from 14 to 19 months. For example, one morning she was busily working on a puzzle with a friend when she was told by her mother's interviewer that "Mommy and I are going out for a while." Donna looked up and answered, "Okay." While she worked on the puzzle, she quietly looked at the door and said, "Mama." She did not appear to be distressed or unhappy. Not until she finished the puzzle did she calmly leave the toddler room to visit her mother briefly in the interview room. On another morning the mothers of the four toddlers present in the toddler room were asked to leave the room.

Donna was not bothered by her mother's departure. She occasionally said, "Mommy," and looked at her mother's photograph, but she did not need to go to her mother. She played more freely with adults and peers than she had when her mother was in the room. She often mothered her dolls and other children, and she followed "rules," for example, to stay in the toddler room and to behave in a grown-up manner. These "rules" were her understanding of her mother's expectations.

Donna's ability to tolerate her mother's absences better than her peers did theirs did not, however, protect her from once again regressing and developing the same symptoms and inhibitions following a urinary infection at 29 months that she had had after her illness at 19 months. The main source of her conflict with her mother at this time was her anger about the verbally stated sense that she did not have a penis. This had played a less important role in her anger at 19 months. She recovered between 32 and 36 months as she had between 25 and 29 months and once again was better able to tolerate her mother's absences than were her peers. Her sense of comfort seemed to rest on the existence of a mental representation of the mother that was relatively secure and stable.

In order to recover and attain a measure of object constancy at 25 and 32 months, it was necessary for Donna to resolve conflicts between her wishes and her mother's prohibitions and to manage to tolerate ambivalence, primarily by means of identification with her mother. The advances that made this possible included the development of representational intelligence, particularly symbolic play and language; improved reality testing; greater tolerance for frustration and anxiety; an ability to postpone and to accept substitute gratification; and the integration of the good and bad aspects of the maternal representation. As a result of these changes and the resolution of conflict, she became better able to tolerate separation, disappointment, and anger. Frustrating experiences with her mother were counteracted by memories of her loving and comforting behavior (Pine 1974).

Most important, Donna began to learn to comfort herself by identifying with her mother's behavior. She began to mother her dolls and express empathy as early as 13 months. By 16 months she used symbolic play with dolls to comfort herself during her mother's absences. The play was an exact replication of the actual mother–child relationship.

Donna not only mothered her dolls but helped the teacher in the toddler room set the table for a party, just as she helped her mother at home. She also encouraged children to come to the table in a motherly and forceful manner, saying, for example, "Come on, Tommy, sit." At 33 months one of the observers wrote: "Once the mother leaves, not only can Donna cope and manage quite well, but she seems to become completely identified with the mother, and she becomes very motherly to other children, and very much aware of what they are doing."

In order to resolve her conflict over aggression, Donna identified with her mother's behavior toward her, behavior that was in part shaped by the mother's resolution of her own conflict over aggression by reaction formation. Identification served many other purposes: by becoming like her mother, by carrying an image of the mother inside her, Donna was able to maintain a tie with the mother internally; and by being like her mother she felt proud of herself. Donna not only identified with her mother's maternal qualities, she also identified with her mother's prohibitions. By identifying with rules of conduct and expectations, Donna was able to be more grown up, to remain in the toddler room, and to organize activities for other children. These accomplishments gave her pleasure. Most important, by identifying with her mother, she also began to get over her unhappiness at not having a penis.

The advances in Donna's development in the third year suggest criteria in addition to the tolerance of separation for evaluating the attainment of object constancy. We saw a shift from need-satisfying, demanding, and clinging relationships to more mature, ego-determined object relations. Indications of this shift included the expression of affection and trust, regard for the interests and feelings of others, the ability to play cooperatively, and the capacity to be concerned (A. Freud 1965). On the same morning that Donna aggressively took a toy from another child, when that child was upset because her mother had left the room, Donna was sympathetic, showed concern, and soothed the child by offering a toy. She valued and treated other children with consideration (see Burgner and Edgcumbe 1972, Sandler and Joffe 1966).

Donna was one of sixteen subjects seen in follow-up studies at the ages of 9 and 25 years. Although she continued to be shy, reserved, and inhibited, as she had been at 19 and 29 months, she was warm, empathic, introspective, and had the capacity to care and to form close and meaningful relationships. The attainment of object constancy persisted, as did the identification with the caretaking functions of the mother (McDevitt 1991).

The boys in the study developed object constancy in the same way Donna did, up to the middle of the rapprochement subphase. Then they began to move away both physically and psychologically from their mothers; they turned toward their fathers, toward father substitutes, and toward more masculine, phallic, aggressive activities and play. Identification with the mother was replaced gradually by identification with the father. For these developments to occur required the mother's encouragement and the father's availability. It seems likely that identification with the father helped the boys to resolve conflicts and ambivalence and attain some measure of object constancy, just as identification with the mother had in the girls.

CLINICAL MATERIAL

I illustrate the clinical usefulness of the concept of object constancy with two cases, first of a 3-year-old girl and then of an adult woman. Reconstructions in these cases were facilitated by my understanding of the effects of failure to achieve object constancy.

Becky

In contrast to Donna, Becky had a less fortunate development. She began analysis at the age of 3, after having developed a severe problem separating from her mother and a fear of being bitten by a witch or a mustached man, a few months earlier (McDevitt 1971). She clung to her mother, appeared sad and anxious, cried inconsolably, and insisted that her mother stay with her at all times. At bedtime, she demanded that she be allowed to sleep with or near the mother, or else that the mother maintain a constant vigil by her bedside. She awoke frequently during the night and ran to her parents' bed. Her fear (expressed verbally, in dreams, and in anxious clinging) was that her mother might leave her and never return. She also frequently whined, complained, provoked, and fought with her mother. In the analysis, however, she showed excessive concern and love for her mother, who became the "good" object, and aggression toward the analyst, who became the "bad" object. In one session, after attacking the boy doll's penis, Becky suddenly decided to go to her mother in the waiting room, as she often did. When she nuzzled up to her mother, she meant to say that she wanted her mother to come into the office. Instead, she said that she wanted her mother to die. Recognizing her slip, she insisted that her mother come to the office. Although she made an effort to be nice and to make up, she continued to express her anger by caring for her mother in an overbearing and annoying manner (McDevitt 1967).

Becky's dread of being abandoned by her mother was a consequence of death wishes directed toward and projected into her mother. Although the immediate reasons for these wishes were a highly charged oedipal situation, penis envy, and sibling rivalry, they had their roots in a disturbed mother–child interaction characteristic of the entire preoedipal phase. Becky's fear of being bitten by a mustached man represented a fear of oral and genital impulses directed toward and projected into the father.

Becky and her mother got off to a bad start because as an infant Becky cried frequently and was difficult to comfort. She was hypersensitive, tense, and slept poorly. The mother, who had looked forward to an academic career, resented Becky's demands and felt unhappy and inadequate as a mother. She alternated between being overly permissive and, after a long buildup of anger while attempting tolerance, exploding and sometimes hitting Becky or withdrawing from her emotionally and, occasionally, physically by going into another room.

By 8 months Becky showed marked stranger and separation anxiety. Her practicing subphase, from 10 to 16 months, was subdued and lacking in the elation characteristic of that stage. In the rapprochement subphase, from 18 to 24 months, after her mother had withdrawn emotionally and had turned over Becky's care almost completely to a strict and dominating maid, Becky's separation anxiety became acute once again, and she developed a severe sleep disturbance. During the fourth subphase, from 24 to 36 months, Becky continued to show heightened ambivalence, excessive separation anxiety, and a depressed, angry, and anxious mood.

The emotional unavailability of the mother during the need–satisfying stage had interfered with the development of basic trust, which can be thought of as the start of the transfer (internalization) of the mother's availability from her actual presence to her intrapsychic representation. In addition, the representation of the mother was ambivalently cathected with an excess of insufficiently fused aggression, bringing about a dearth of tender feelings. Becky was intolerant of frustration and, like her parents, had little control over or tolerance of her impulses. She showed marked conflicts of loyalty, and used the defense mechanism of splitting of the object representation during the early months of her analysis.

Becky had not shown evidence of identification with her mother prior to or during her illness, as Donna had. Instead, there was a continuous struggle with the real and with the introjected mother. The latter was then projected into the external world in the form of a witch. This failure in identification with a loving maternal representation left Becky lacking in confidence, unhappy with herself, and fearful of her impulses. This condition was in contrast to Donna's identification, which boosted her self-esteem and played a major role in helping her to resolve conflicts.

Becky's object representation, as compared with Donna's, was more tenuous, ambivalently cathected, and unstable. The failure in both the development of object constancy and in identification increased her vulnerability to severe conflicts during the phallic-oedipal phase. The increased aggression directed toward the mother at that time became all the more dangerous in view of Becky's doubts with regard to the mother's physical and emotional availability—doubts that now had their basis in the uncertain inner representation of the mother. These doubts increased Becky's fear of object loss and thereby predisposed her to the development—in part, the reactivation—of intense anxiety on any occasion of threatened separation from her mother. Her long history of separation anxiety had "sensitized" Becky to the experience of separation. Intense fear of object loss had persisted and was now involved in the internalized conflicts of the phallic-oedipal phase.

Mrs. A.

Mrs. A. had a more difficult childhood and a more severe illness than Becky did. She began analysis at the age of 43 because of alcoholism, severe depression, sexual inhibitions, and social anxiety. She had had severe emotional problems since childhood, had made several suicide attempts, and had been hospitalized. It was difficult for her to feel comfortable or to talk freely: her feelings were too intense; she was constantly buffeted between strong impulses and a punitive superego; and she found it difficult to separate fantasy from reality, inner from outer, past from present. I not only reminded her of her parents, I was her parents. Her severe depressions were the result of uncontrollable rage turned inward by a harsh and cruel superego that attacked her with the "voices" of her parents, primarily her mother's. These voices were often attributed to me, as were sexually exciting derivatives of a beating fantasy in which she imagined my attacking, hurting, criticizing, deserting, and leaving her. She could not smoke in my presence, look at me, or read the magazines in my waiting room because these activities stood for fellatio.

She had always experienced separation as rejection and abandonment. Anticipating separation brought on depression. No matter how brief, separations in the analysis made it difficult for her to remember me or to have a friendly or helpful memory of me. Her memory of me was too laden with painful, jealous, and angry feelings. She felt unloved and unwanted. In addition, she felt excitement. Being left meant being hurt, and being hurt was masochistically exciting. She retreated to her room, drank, and repeated autoerotic fantasies and activities from childhood.

Once, after seeing a beautiful piece of sculpture, which she could remember in great detail afterward, she realized that she could not remember me easily. Our relationship was too painful. It reminded her too much of her mother. If she phoned her mother, she never knew what to expect. She could count on a relationship to a piece of sculpture (as she had been able to with a bottle of whiskey before she gave up drinking), but she could not count on me or keep an image of me in her mind. When with me, though she wanted to look at me, she was afraid that looking would give rise to sexually exciting, painful, jealous, or angry feelings. After her son went to camp, she could no longer remember what he looked like. She was angry because she felt deserted, so angry she did not want him to return.

On one occasion, in anticipation of a separation, she said that she wanted to look at me, to drink me in, that she was addicted to me. She added that she had never really had a mother, and she presumed that having a mother was necessary. She then went to the bathroom to vomit, "to vomit you up" (meaning *me*).

Prior to my vacations it was necessary for me to give Mrs. A. something of mine, usually a book. During vacation it was necessary for me to keep in touch with her regularly by phone. Otherwise she found it difficult to have a positive and reliable memory of me. She told me that she had never been able to describe her mother. She could not picture her or understand what kind of woman she was. She had no difficulty, however, maintaining a positive image of her father.

Being left meant not only loss and excitement but also castration. In one session before my vacation she recalled that prior to a tonsillectomy at age 4 she felt a lump with her tongue. Afterward, she felt a hole. She then spoke of discovering her vagina when she was between 2 and 3. Separation made her think that something was wrong with her, that she was different, that no one would like her or want to be with her or see her. She realized that her fellatio fantasy had the purpose of getting semen, which, like glue, would put her back together again. She referred to a doll from childhood that had fallen apart. She felt like that doll, as if she were falling apart. She didn't know where her arms were, or where her head was. In another session prior to a vacation she felt sexual excitement in the mouth and vagina, wanted to grab and tear off my penis and swallow it in order to feel whole again.

Mrs. A. had suffered unusual deprivation, trauma, and abuse throughout her childhood. The mother was self-absorbed, sarcastic, and critical. She was not reliable or affectionate and cared little for children. The father, although more caring and maternal, overstimulated and seduced her. He also used her. He would cease exciting play with her to talk with a woman on the phone or go to a party. He encouraged the mother to have many lovers in the home. In this atmosphere the patient developed a strong sense of guilt and a puritanical attitude toward sex.

The parents took frequent trips lasting for months, and the patient never knew when they would return. She was brought up by servants who constantly changed. She did not recall being attached to any of them. She reacted to her parents' absences after the age of 9 by giving herself enemas to relieve her loneliness; these led to her becoming excited, followed by going to sleep.

These childhood events posed a problem for the analysis because the patient was convinced that in her analysis she would have sexual relations with me. She was extremely jealous of my patients and believed that I had impregnated one of them.

Mrs. A. repeated in the transference the same vivid feelings, fantasies, and physical symptoms that had accompanied exciting experiences and trauma in her past. Her wish was to re-experience with me the close, sexual encounters she had had with her father. Guilt in the form of "voices," which were also projected into me, were the critical voices of her mother. She had many dreams of sexual relations with me followed by other dreams of being severely punished.

Mrs. A.'s conflicts were not only phallic-oedipal. In addition to an intense urge to put my penis in her mouth or vagina to get semen (glue) in order to keep her from falling apart, to fill up holes and repair defects, she also wanted to put me in her vagina and keep me there. She said she could not live without me. When she had these urges she felt excitement in the mouth and the vagina. By keeping me inside her, she could be assured of my closeness and availability. These wishes for closeness were associated with wishes to be close to her mother, to get in her lap, wishes that were rarely fulfilled. They were also associated with feeling comfortable and whole when on trips with her father, neither guilty nor fearful, except when he made sexual advances and she "blanked out." Because of her highly ambivalent relationship with her mother, like Becky she was not able to satisfactorily identify with her. She was much closer to and more like her father. She shared many of his interests, which led to important sublimations as she improved in the analysis.

She was afraid of her wish to be too close to me, of being glued to me like a stamp to an envelope. To be too close not only caused her to feel guilty, she also feared it would cause me to lose part of myself or frighten me so much that I would jump out of the window. Separation or too great a distance was also frightening. She would not only lose me but also part of herself. She had to maintain an optimal distance. Although she reacted appropriately to her father's death in the fourth year of the analysis, the transference continued to be by far the most important concern in her life.

Her need for me, her sexual urges, became even more intense months before vacations. She would begin to feel depressed, helpless, unable to call friends or engage in her usual activities. She also became hurt and angry, imagining me with another woman, and threatened to drink, commit suicide, get another doctor, in order to coerce me and prevent me from leaving.

Another problem with closeness was a conflict of loyalties. This sounded like the ambivalent conflicts present during the rapprochement crisis. She was torn between being loyal to me on the one hand and her wishes to involve herself with other people and other activities on the other. If she followed the latter course, she feared that I, like her mother, would punish her. She wondered how she could sometimes love and other times hate me so intensely.

Mrs. A. was not able to maintain a constant or reliable memory of the absent love object. This inability had been present as long as she could remember. The memory of the absent person was too burdened with violent, poorly modulated, sexual, and aggressive impulses about which she felt intense guilt. Deprivation, trauma, and abuse during her first three years created a disturbance in the nature of the cathexis of the representation of the love object and in the quality of that representation. As a consequence, she did not have the opportunity to establish a reliable and consistent image of her mother. As was the case with Becky, a failure in the attainment of object constancy led to severe conflicts in the phallic-oedipal phase and to a severe depressive-masochistic character disorder with hysterical symptoms.

DISCUSSION

There seems to be disagreement about the clinical use of object constancy similar to the disagreement about whether it begins to be attained in the first or in the third year.

If we leave aside severely disturbed institutionalized and some psychotic children, the patients referred to in the literature reviewed and those described in this paper had developed a specific libidinal attachment to the love object. And, aside from Adler and Buie's (1979) view of borderline patients, they had also acquired evocative memory.

There was no evidence that Mrs. A. or Becky had a cognitive defect in evocative memory. Mrs. A. did show signs of what Pine (1979) calls pathology in relation to the undifferentiated other, for example, panic accompanying fantasies of merging and separateness. This panic occurred primarily in the context of an emotionally charged transference, much less in her everyday life. It seemed to be the result of regressive fantasies rather than a cognitive disturbance in self–object differentiation.

The most important factor interfering with the attainment of object constancy referred to in the literature reviewed, and in Donna, Becky, and Mrs. A., was the incapacity to maintain a stable libidinal object representation, whether as a result of a failure to establish a firm libidinal object in the first year (the institutionalized children) or in the context of resolving the ambivalence and conflicts characteristic of the rapprochement subphase in the third year.

We can illustrate the difference between the two views of the development and meaning of object constancy by referring again to the severely disturbed neurotic and borderline children described by Edgcumbe and Burgner (1972). Even though they appeared to be in the need-satisfying stage, they were said to have progressed to the beginning attainment of object constancy, since the aim of the regression was to bind the object to the child more firmly. If the authors had used Mahler's definition, they might have concluded that some of these children had not progressed to the beginning attainment of object constancy, since the fears of destroying or losing the object or the object's love, which caused the regression, were the fears and conflicts typical of the rapprochement crisis. Indeed, the authors described a young adolescent girl who had never resolved her conflict over feelings of ambivalence to her mother early in life and had remained excessively demanding of the mother for love and attention.

Edgcumbe and Burgner's view accords with remarks made by Anna Freud at a 1968 Panel. Anna Freud described how a little girl, age 4 or 5, explained why it was so important to have a photograph of her mother. She said, "That is so that you don't think they have gone all nasty when you haven't seen them for a long time." Anna Freud went on to say, "Now this isn't quite what object constancy means, because the aggressive or angry relation to the object is still a relationship . . . . the next step would be to lose the object altogether, because it has given disappointment, pain, and frustration. But one is tied to it good or bad, for better or worse. I think that is object constancy" (p. 507). In other words, as long as the specific libidinal attachment to the mother, which had its beginning in the first year of life, persists, she considers object constancy to exist irrespective of the nature of the cathexis of the tie or the quality of the representation.

In order to examine more clearly different views of changes in the nature or quality of object cathexis, I will quote Anna Freud (1952) again. "I developed the idea that the step from the first to the second stage of object relationship—from the *milieu interne* to the psychological object (Hoffer), from the need-satisfying object to object constancy (Hartmann), from part objects to whole objects (Melanie Klein)—is determined by a decrease in the urgency of the drives themselves . . . While the infant is under the full impact of his needs. . . . he demands from the object only one thing: that is immediate satisfaction. . . . The needs have to lessen in strength, or have to be brought under ego control before nonsatisfying (for instance, absent) objects can retain their cathexis" (pp. 233–234). She writes that when Hoffer describes a transformation of narcissistic into object libido, Hartmann makes the more far-reaching assumption of a change from instinctual to neutralized cathexis. Both consider the shift to object constancy to be accomplished by changes in the quality of object cathexis, in contrast to Anna Freud's view, which leans toward a quantitative explanation.

Hartmann (1952) wrote, "This constancy probably pre-supposes on the side of the ego a certain neutralization of aggressive as well as libidinal energy" (p. 163). He thought that neutralization was mediated by the ego, that there was an interrelationship between the instinctual and the ego aspects of object relations, and that object constancy both influenced and was dependent on ego development. In 1966 Mahler wrote, "It is the mother's love and acceptance of the toddler and even of his ambivalence which enables the toddler's ego to cathect his self-representation with 'neutralized' energy" (p. 161), a statement equally applicable to the toddler's ability to cathect the object representation with "neutralized" energy.

Sandler and Joffe (1966) emphasize the role of the ego in the development of object constancy. The object not only provides sexual satisfaction but is valued, loved, and cared for. The object is invested with an ego-determined enduring and affective attachment cathexis. It may be helpful to think of affective value cathexis beginning in the first year with the specific attachment to the mother and continuing into the third year and beyond with the more complex relationships and identifications with other love objects.

Mahler's view (1965, Mahler et al. 1975) adds to these quantitative and qualitative changes in object cathexis other changes that do not begin to be completed until the end of the third year. In her view the establishment of object constancy depends on the gradual internalization of a constant, posi-tively cathected inner image of the mother. She wrote (Mahler et al. 1975). "But the constancy of the object implies more than the maintenance of the representation of the absent love object. It also implies the unifying of the 'good' and the 'bad' object into one whole representation. This fosters the fusion of the aggressive and libidinal drives and tempers the hatred for the object when aggression is intense" (p. 110). She thought, like Hartmann, that the state of object constancy had a special bearing on the fate of the aggressive and hostile drives. When she wrote, "In the state of object constancy, the love object will not be rejected or exchanged for another if it cannot provide satisfaction; and in that state, the object is still longed for and not rejected (hated) as unsatisfactory simply because of its absence" (p. 110), her emphasis was on the tolerance of aggression, not just on the libidinal tie to the mother.

Blum (1981) noted that intrapsychic separateness and the resolution of ambivalence are interdependent. In "object inconstancy" the child will deny the object's independent existence and substitute a persecutory, aggressive (part) object relationship for the missing positively toned object constancy.

In Mahler's view the senior toddler must not only resolve the ambivalence typical of the rapprochement subphase but also the interpersonal and intrapsychic conflicts in his or her relationship with the mother.

Hartmann, following Freud, wrote in 1955 that neutralization is closely related to identification. As we have seen in Donna's development, another important factor in the attainment of object constancy is identification with the mother. Identification plays a major role in modifying the quality of object cathexis.

Unlike Becky and Mrs. A. who had too little "neutralized" cathexis and too little affective value cathexis, Donna used the ego mechanism of identification to tame aggression, to resolve the ambivalence and conflicts in her rapprochement crisis, and to add to her ego-determined value cathexis of the object. The latter was seen in her concern for and care of dolls and other children. The uncertain and unreliable quality of the maternal representation in Becky and Mrs. A. was based on deprivation, trauma, and a disturbed relationship with the mother, which had interfered with their use of identification to resolve ambivalence and conflicts.

Identification contributes not only to constant object relations, it also contributes to ego development, self-esteem, and self-constancy. When Donna was enmeshed in conflict with her mother, she clung to her, sadly and helplessly. She was not able to engage in doll play. When she overcame the rapprochement crisis, she became self-assured and outgoing, in part by identifying with her mother, by becoming a little mother to dolls and to younger children.

It may be useful to think of degrees of attainment of object constancy and to think of its attainment as a continuing process. The fact that Donna was able to attain a high degree of object constancy did not prevent her from developing the same symptoms she had during the rapprochement crisis when she developed a castration crisis, nor did it prevent the same symptoms from persisting at the age of 25. Becky failed to a marked degree to attain object constancy, Donna to a minor degree. Although Donna's object relations were stable and loving, they were somewhat burdened by her inhibitions and a tendency to involve herself in disappointing relationships with men. In other words, the difficulty she had managing aggression, which was connected with aspects of her maternal representation, and which subsequently became the superego, interfered to a degree with the quality of her object relationships.

CONCLUSION

With the acquisition of constant object representations, the child gains greater autonomy from the love object, from the sensorimotor actions in which the child was formerly embedded, and to some degree from drive and conflict, and from

regressive tendencies. Since this autonomy is relative, however, the constancy of the object representation fluctuates
depending on wish, anxiety and depressive affect, and on
defense. It is a compromise formation, a consequence of psychic conflict. The stability of Donna's representation of her
mother fluctuated. During stable periods the compromise
formation was successful, during periods of regression it was
not. In each of the analyses presented, as the capacity for
constant object relations became more stable, the patient's
condition improved. When Donna's ambivalence and conflicts were resolved, her object representation became more
stable.

Object constancy does not become a component of subsequent conflict as does the superego, but it does provide
some assurance against anxiety and depressive affect, and it
contributes to ego development. Becky's, and Mrs. A.'s, unstable object constancy made it difficult for them to tolerate
frustration and ambivalence, anxiety and conflict, or to develop signal anxiety. In contrast to Donna, their conflicts
were more pervasive and disruptive, and were dealt with by
the use of more primitive defense mechanisms. The protective
quality of a constant object representation was augmented in
Donna by identification with that representation. Donna not
only identified with the comforting qualities of the representation of her mother (Furer 1967), probably a precursor to the
ego ideal, she also identified with her mother's standards of
behavior and prohibitions—precursors to the superego.

I have examined the concept of object constancy by
reviewing the literature and by correlating data obtained by
the direct observation of children with analytic data. There are
two views of the concept. One refers to it as the capacity to
maintain object cathexis irrespective of gratification or frustration. The other stresses, in addition, the need for the ego to
resolve the ambivalence and conflicts characteristic of the
rapprochement subphase. This resolution is brought about by

ego mechanisms, particularly that of identification with the mother (and, in boys, also the father). I suggest that the second view is the more useful one. The more or less successful resolution of the rapprochement crisis and attainment of object constancy set the stage for the more or less successful resolution of the conflicts typical of the phallic–oedipal phase, to a considerable extent by use of identification leading to the formation of the superego.

REFERENCES

Adler, G., and Buie, Jr., D. H. (1979). Aloneness and borderline psychopathology: the possible relevance of child development issues. *International Journal of Psycho-Analysis* 60:83–96.

Blum, H. P. (1981). Object inconstancy and paranoid conspiracy. *Journal of the American Psychoanalytic Association* 29:789–813.

Burgner, M., and Edgcumbe, R. (1972). Some problems in the conceptualization of early object relations. Part 2. The concept of object constancy. *Psychoanalytic Study of the Child* 27:315–333. New York: Quadrangle Books.

Edgcumbe, R., and Burgner, M. (1972). Some problems in the conceptualization of early object relationships. Part 1. The concepts of need satisfaction and need-satisfying relationships. *Psychoanalytic Study of the Child* 27:283–314. New York: Quadrangle Books.

Fleming, J. (1975). Some observations on object constancy in the psychoanalysis of adults. *Journal of the American Psychoanalytic Association* 23:743–761.

Fraiberg, S. (1969). Object constancy and mental representation. *Psychoanalytic Study of the Child* 24:9–47. New York: International Universities Press.

Frank, A. (1992). A problem with the couch: incapacities and conflicts. In *When the Body Speaks*, ed. S. Kramer and S. Akhtar, pp. 90–112. Northvale, NJ: Jason Aronson.

Freud, A. (1952). Mutual influence of ego and id. In *The Writings of Anna Freud*, vol. 6, pp. 230–244. New York: International Universities Press, 1968.

——— (1965). *Normality and Pathology in Childhood. The Writings of Anna Freud*, vol. 6. New York: International Universities Press.

Furer, M. (1967). Some developmental aspects of the superego. *International Journal of Psycho-Analysis* 48:277–290.

Galenson, E., and Roiphe, H. (1971). The impact of early sexual discovery on mood, defensive organization, and symbolization. *Psychoanalytic Study of the Child* 26:195–216. New York: Quadrangle Books.

Gyomroi, E. L. (1963). The analysis of a young concentration camp victim. *Psychoanalytic Study of the Child* 18:484–510. New York: International Universities Press.

Hartmann, H. (1952). The mutual influences in the development of ego and id. In *Essays on Ego Psychology*, pp. 155–182. New York: International Universities Press, 1964.

_____ (1955). Notes on the theory of sublimation. In *Essays on Ego Psychology*. New York: International Universities Press, 1964.

Kernberg, O. F. (1975). *Borderline Conditions and Pathological Narcissism*. New York: Jason Aronson.

Mahler, M. S. (1965). On the significance of the normal separation-individuation phase with reference to research in symbiotic child psychosis. In *Drives, Affects, Behavior*, vol. 2, ed. M. Schur, pp. 161–169. New York: International Universities Press.

_____ (1966). Notes on the development of basic moods: the depressive affect. In *Psychoanalysis—A General Psychology: Essays in Honor of Heinz Hartmann*, ed. R. Loewenstein, L. Newman, M. Schur, and A. Solnit. New York: International Universities Press.

_____ (1968) (in collaboration with Furer, M.). *On Human Symbiosis and the Vicissitudes of Individuation*. New York: International Universities Press.

Mahler, M. S., Pine, F., and Bergman, A. (1975). *The Psychological Birth of the Human Infant: Symbiosis and Individuation*. New York: Basic Books.

McDevitt, J. B. (1967). A separation problem in a 3-year-old girl. In *The Child Analyst at Work*, ed. E. R. Geleerd, pp. 24–58. New York: International Universities Press.

_____ (1971). Pre-oedipal determinants of an infantile neurosis. In *Separation-Individuation: Essays in Honor of Margaret S. Mahler*, ed. J. B. McDevitt and C. F. Settlage, pp. 201–226. New York: International Universities Press.

_____ (1975). Separation-individuation and object constancy. *Journal of the American Psychoanalytic Association* 23(4):713–742.

_____ (1991). Contributions of separation-individuation theory to the understanding of psychopathology during the prelatency years. In *Beyond the Symbiotic Orbit: Advances in Separation-Individuation: Essays in Honor of Selma Kramer, M.D.*, ed. S. Akhtar and H. Parens, pp. 153–169. Hillsdale, NJ: Analytic Press.

Panel (1968). Panel discussion. J. A. Arlow, moderator. *International Journal of Psycho-Analysis* 49:506–512.

Piaget, J. (1937). *The Construction of Reality in the Child*. New York: Basic Books, 1954.

Pine, F. (1974). Libidinal object constancy: a theoretical note. *Psychoanalysis and Contemporary Science* 3:307–313.

_____ (1979). Pathology of the separation-individuation process as manifested in later clinical work. *International Journal of Psycho-Analysis* 60:225–242.

Roiphe, H. (1968). On an early genital phase: with an addendum on genesis. *Psychoanalytic Study of the Child* 23:348–365. New York: International Universities Press.

Sandler, J., and Joffe, W. G. (1966). On skill and sublimation. *Journal of the American Psychoanalytic Association* 14:335–355.

Solnit, A. J. (1982). Developmental perspectives on self and object constancy. *Psychoanalytic Study of the Child* 37:201–218. New Haven, CT: Yale University Press.

Spitz, R. A., and Cobliner, W. G. (1965). *The First Year*. New York: International Universities Press.

3

MAPPING OUT THE INTERNAL WORLD

Four Discussions of McDevitt's Chapter "The Concept of Object Constancy and Its Clinical Applications"

Eva Berberich, M.D.
Anni Bergman, Ph.D.
Paul L. Janssen, M.D.
Helen C. Meyers, M.D.

CONSTANCY OF THE OBJECT
by Eva Berberich, M.D.

In Chapter 2, John McDevitt focuses on the clinical applications of the concept of object constancy, citing clinical examples, among them the cases of two children, Donna and Becky.

The significance of identification in the attainment of object constancy is demonstrated by the case of Donna. The close, mutually satisfying relation between the mother and her baby in the first months of life seems to be of greatest importance. The positive character of this relation presumably was the basis for the relative equilibrium between aggressive and libidinal forces in Donna's later life. The capacity of the child to tolerate ambivalence on the basis of identification with the mother is demonstrated impressively, as Donna is able to tame her frustrating experiences by means of memories of her mother's caring and soothing behavior. Evaluating the attainment of object constancy is measured not only through tolerance of separation but also through the development of more mature, ego-determined object relations, regard for the feelings of others, expression of trust, ability to cooperate in play, and the capacity for concern and for reparation. For the European reader the expression "capacity for concern" is not, as McDevitt saw it, connected with Anna Freud (1965) but with Winnicott and "The Development of the Capacity for Concern" (1963).

The clinical usefulness of the concept of object constancy is demonstrated by the case of Becky and the case of a 43-year-old woman. The case of Becky is already well known because the author reported this treatment on another occasion. She began her analysis when she was 3 years old.

In contrast to Donna, Becky and her mother had a bad start, devoid of any joyful mutuality. In consequence, the developmental phases that followed were full of tension, and the relation between mother and child remained extremely fragile, dominated by outbursts of unbound aggression. The mother remained an inconstant object for Becky, who regarded her as a persecutory object (witch) to be controlled. Nor, interestingly, did Becky find a transitional object. Insufficient and insecure representations were the result of this derailed development, with no sign of identification with the loving maternal object.

Mrs. A, the adult patient, also had a difficult childhood. Among other difficulties, she was incapable of keeping an internal image of objects during separation. So, adapting to the patient's needs in a way that is well known from child analysis, McDevitt would give her something of his, a book, for instance, and would keep in touch with her during vacations by telephone. This case was otherwise remarkable because of the parallelism between loss of object representation and loss of self-representation. The patient herself found an impressive metaphor for describing her feeling of self-fragmentation that corresponds with separation, castration, and finally with death: she referred to a doll from childhood that had fallen apart. The overwhelming parents, the sequence of separation, fragmentation of object and self-representation, and fear of castration and death was recapitulated in the transference, which, as McDevitt puts it, "continued to be by far the most important concern in her life."

SOME REFLECTIONS

Although the concept of object constancy has for many years been extensively discussed in our institutes especially where seminars on children are held—in the context of the study of the works of Mahler (1967, 1974, Mahler et al. 1975), it has not acquired the same significance in the German literature as it has among our American colleagues. We use the term *constancy* more in the sense of constant object relations that are the result of object constancy.

My own account of the treatment of a mother and baby in which the child's age and psychopathology closely resembled that of Becky, may contribute something else to the discussion, both from the point of view of object constancy in the child and in connection with the increasing constancy of the object. I am referring here to integrative and structuring processes in the mother. The latter was at first subject to massive fluctuations in her behavior as well as in her basic attitude to the child and in the fantasies that helped to mold her behavior. As a result, the child was exposed to what might be described as an enormous and constantly changing field of tension. Unlike Becky, and notwithstanding what seems to me to be perhaps an even more unfavorable initial situation, the child developed very well in the period of therapy between the tenth month and the third year of her life.

The Case of Lili

The initial interview with Lili—10 months old—and her mother already gave sufficient indication of the degree of distressing asynchrony between the two and of the absence of mutuality in their bodily experience. This was entirely consistent with what I soon learned about the emotional mismatch between the mother and child, which had been present from the beginning. Immediately after the birth, when shown her little daughter for the first time, the mother had felt a kind of shock on seeing her: "That is not what you imagined; that is not your double, it is someone else's child." She was horrified to see that the child bore such a close resemblance to her husband's family. She also experienced the birth as the loss of something that had been very important to her: the perfect unity between herself and the child in her womb.

It was therefore impossible for any true mutuality to arise between Lili and her mother. The mother was unable to breast-feed her baby. She behaved clumsily and restlessly, and was unable to empathize, to "read the signals," as she put it; the child remained alien to her. Nor did she enjoy holding her in her arms or looking after her and caring for her; by the age of only 3 months, she had put her in a high chair for feeding. Lili was difficult to feed from the beginning. She seemed not to be hungry at all, and would simply turn her head aside and react with indifference. These reactions came to a head between the third and sixth months of Lili's life (after an infection of the urinary tract). The mother described how she would shout at Lili, try to open her mouth by force, or use the television to distract her before stuffing food into her mouth in the form of a surprise attack. If the little girl then refused to accede to the mother's wishes, the mother would become furious, feel intense hatred, go into fits of rage, and not want to have anything more to do with her. "Then I just wanted her out of the way, or dead," she said. As if in passing, she then mumbled something that sounded like "kill her off."

When Lili was 6 months old, her feeding problems were accompanied by severe sleep disorders and fits of screaming, which the parents could cope with only by giving her sedatives. The mother was now utterly disappointed at having such an imperfect child, in whom she could see only defects and other negative attributes. And she was by now hardly able to control her increasing fear that the child might contract an intestinal infection or have a hereditary intestinal disease, from which she might die. (As a former pediatrician, the mother had been a specialist in hereditary diseases of the gut.)

Sometimes, however, she felt upset at the sight of her crying child because she was perfectly aware that Lili was not crying out of rage but as if in deep despair. Occasionally, she would see tears running down her daughter's cheeks as she slept, "as if she were having a nightmare." This may well have been not far from the truth, as the first dream later reported by Lili suggests.

Mrs. X. displayed an extreme narcissistic vulnerability combined with a disappointment in herself that a healthy, lusty baby with no problems was intended to help overcome. Then at least, she often thought, there would have been something positive in her life. When Lili's difficulties at 6 months seemed to have no end, the mother's relationship with her little daughter underwent an abrupt change: from that point on she projected only negative parts of herself into the child, as Lili had proved unfit to fill her narcissistic void. Mrs. X. was horrified at the intensity of her wish to be rid of the child. Sometimes when she left her in the care of friends or the family, she would forget all about her. She also often thought of having Lili adopted. She would then conclude, "You must admit that I am a monster, a particularly wicked monster."

Mrs. X. brought Lili along regularly to the sessions, two

times a week, and sometimes also attempted to feed her in my presence. In so doing, she gave way to every refusal, however feeble, by the child, as she could not tolerate any protest; yet disavowing her destructive impulses aroused in her nearly uncontrollable rage. On one occasion when we were talking about this, she mentioned that during the course of her professional career an adolescent patient had committed suicide, and that she had experienced this as the result of an attempt by her to get her own way with this young man.

For her part, the child, sensing the fragility of the relationship, did not dare to defend herself aggressively against her mother's wishes. Instead, I noticed on many occasions that she would bite her own arm violently in situations that must have aroused anger at her mother. Nor did Lili respond with annoyance to prohibitions by her mother, but rather with inconsolable crying, together with a desire to be taken into her mother's arms immediately—indicating that she experienced every "no" as signifying a total loss of love. But most of the time the mother had difficulties in saying "no" and showed a considerable lack of firmness, a result of her anger and disappointment. So Lili could identify neither with mother's caring capability nor with mother's no-saying capabilities.

One day Mrs. X. reported indignantly that at home Lili, now 15 months old, would deliberately fall out of her high chair. As it happens, she kept on falling over anyway, and would appear at the sessions with bruises and scratches. Annoyed and uncomprehending, the mother called this behavior silly, and in any case often thought that she had a silly, stupid child who was not quite right in the head. Since Lili had been looking at me with wide-open eyes while the mother was telling me this, I gave her the following explanation: "I suppose you are often afraid that you might get lost. You are not sure if Mummy is always keeping an eye on you properly or if she might perhaps let you fall."

Lili listened to my words without any apparent change of

facial expression. Shortly afterward, she began to jump up and down on the couch—something I saw as a manifestation of joy and well-being. Now she grabbed hold of a teddy bear she had previously brought in from the children's therapy room and threw it to me. I felt that she expected me to throw it back to her, and I did so. With a cry of joy, Lili tried to catch it, and threw it back to me again. All of a sudden she seemed like a normal, happy little girl, and we both enjoyed the game that had started up so unexpectedly between us. To forestall the mother's constant criticism, Lili shouted out: "I am silly!"— imitating her mother and almost making fun of her. Without warning, she then deliberately fell off the couch, so that I could only just catch hold of her. It seemed to me as if she had been staging the theme of being dropped and being caught, first with the teddy bear and then, as a repetition, with herself. This successful intervention presumably made it possible for her now to approach the theme of aggression. She showed me a little alligator, which she had also fetched from the children's therapy room and which had gleaming white teeth, saying: "No teeth." I replied: "I imagine you think that little animals and little children mustn't bite when they get annoyed. So it is better if they don't have any teeth in the first place." The mother, however, failed to understand what had taken place between Lili and me, and was ultimately more inclined to think that Lili's eyes should be examined by an ophthalmologist: something must be wrong with her eyes if she could not see the teeth.

When Lili was 20 months old, her mother brought her with her because she was very worried about the child's persistent and extreme reaction to an experience she had had while in the company of her father. The mother had since come to think that her daughter had developed a psychosis. In the presence of the child she told me how, a few days earlier, Lili and her father had taken the family car, which was normally used by Mrs. X. and the child, to the car wash. The two of them, father and daughter, had watched the car disappearing into the car wash. This disappearance of the car induced a totally unpredictable, nameless terror in the child. She screamed and cried and shouted over and over again: "Car, Car, vroom, vroom, Tati, Tati!" (Tati was her pet name for the grandmother she loved so much.) The father felt helpless and, not knowing how to come the child's aid, reacted furiously. To this day it had not been possible to calm the child down, even at home, where she would again and again reenact the washing scene by causing herself to "disappear" into her big doll's house. Over and over again she would call out the same words in terror; and over and over and again, the grandmother had to be telephoned.

While I was still wondering whether the grandmother, like myself as therapist, might represent a third person for Lili outside the mother–child relationship, Lili once again became very agitated. While the mother was talking, she looked for the children's telephones and demanded that Tati be called. I agreed. When this had been done and she had calmed down somewhat, I began to repeat the story once again, just as I had just heard it from the mother. The fact of my having agreed to the telephone call was, I imagine, an important step. It had presumably given Lili the feeling that I was on her side, and that she could count on my support. I then went a step further and explained to Lili that she must have felt very afraid of herself disappearing into the car wash and being swallowed up by it. I took for granted that the car stood for herself, and taking yet another step, I added that she had perhaps also been afraid that she might disappear into her Mummy. She had manifestly felt that only Tati could help her then.

When Lili responded by asking once again for Tati to be called on the telephone, I saw this as a staging of her need to be allowed, and to be able, to call on someone outside the relationship with her mother, and of the hope of being able to secure the mother's approval under the protection of the relationship with me. After a degree of calm had eventually been restored, this time it was Lili who added a new dimension to the scene. Returning from the child's therapy room, to which she had withdrawn, she brought with her two bears tied firmly together, which another child had left there. In considerable agitation, she categorically demanded that the two be separated immediately. (One of the bears, incidentally, was big and the other small.) The meaning of this was perfectly clear between her and me, and we did not say anything more about it.

The experiences in this session—the experience of my presence and the possibility of tolerating and understanding her distress—had clearly been enough to comfort her and encourage her in her demand for help. An explanation of the possible meaning of this experience had been sufficient for her to venture a new step in her development. This was confirmed a few days later when the mother reported that Lili had now chosen her panda as a constant companion and that the sheep, William, an animal from the mother's own childhood, which she had forced on her, had been dropped. At the age of 20 months Lili had found a transitional object. Little by little, I got the impression that Lili was on the way, at least to a certain extent, toward object constancy.

The question for me was why this was the case—why object constancy was able to develop so much more stably. One possible explanation is that I intervened in the mother–child relationship at a very early stage. I know that Eleanor Galenson has been conducting such therapies systematically since the late 1970s, so I imagine my idea must be very familiar to her. The mother was in effect able to catch up on her maturation within the therapeutic relationship, which, although difficult, had a fundamentally positive tinge and in which she was able to experience me as a constant object for herself.

I postulate that the child was imperceptibly able to take

identificatory steps not only with the mother as an object but also with a rapid, positive process of development in the mother. Integrative processes were taking place in the mother, and the child was able to share in the experience of them. The child could perceive Mrs. X. as a mother who was assuming increasing stability. I presume that this was important in the mother–child relationship and that we were able to glimpse what can happen when a child is able to identify with this maternal maturational process and not only with what McDevitt calls the mother's caregiver function.

Increasingly, Lili tried to imitate her mother's behavior, not only in order to overcome her own aggression but also quite consciously as a technique for escaping from her mother's influence and for opposing her verbally. Once again making use of her experiences in the interaction with the therapist, Lili attempted to give her mother the feeling of being a good mother who was worth imitating, while at the same time virtually standing the mother's coerciveness on its head, forcing her to allow her more distance and to let her relate to other children without totally rejecting her. It was astonishing to see the energy with which this still quite small girl began to fight her way resolutely out of this suffocating relationship. Little by little, she had started to make herself independent from a very early age, no longer automatically having her mother look after her, for instance, by changing her own nappies, washing her hair, and so on. She became thoughtful and sensible, helping her mother with the housekeeping. She imitated her mother down to the smallest detail: laying the table, preparing meals, clearing up, filling the dishwasher. In return, she demanded from her mother that the latter take her to playgrounds—that is, to other children— which the mother was usually reluctant to do. Lili would then suggest that she should take over more of the household chores, and the mother found this so touching that she gave way. Sometimes, however, Lili would set off by herself, and she would then be found in someone else's sandpit elsewhere in the neighborhood.

In the session mentioned above, Lili also made breakfast for her mother, for me, and for the panda too, serving up plentiful portions for all and then quickly clearing everything away. The mother watched all this proudly, commenting: "It seems as though I did not make such a mess of everything after all, if Lili wants to grow up to be like me." But she failed to notice the air of joylessness that the scene had for me—its total lack of the quality of play—all of this masked behind Lili's compulsive behavior. Lili again seemed to be imitating her mother almost mockingly, by forcing two little dolls to go to bed in turn, and then snatching them out of bed again, hugging and kissing them and saying affectedly, "But I love you so much." Finally, she painted a creature consisting of a head with arms and legs that the mother indignantly rejected as having been drawn incorrectly. In response, possibly sensing my support, Lili turned to her mother and said, "Don't keep on being so nasty to me, and let me finish when I'm talking!"

Lili was 30 months old when she came for the last time. The mother asked her to tell me a dream she had had the night before. She added—thereby calling the whole thing into question—that she thought Lili had made it up. Lili now told me the dream, saying, "You threw me into the river." She quickly began to draw a river. The mother looked at me with an expression of terror. But Lili went on, totally unruffled, drawing a boat and a helmsman and commenting, as if wishing to weaken the impact, "I made it all up myself." Then, pointing to the helmsman, she said in a mechanical voice, "He is blind."

It is impossible to say whether Lili made it all up for herself or dreamed it. But no matter whether it was a dream or her invention, Lili succeeded in putting into words the nightmare of her life, about which her mother had spoken right at the beginning, thereby indicating that the experience connected with it had attained the level of psychical representability.

With the dream, or rather with the image of being thrown into the river, Lili also verbalized the extent to which she still felt herself to be in danger and to which her psychical integrity in relation to her mother was still at risk. Perhaps she wanted to make it clear to me that I, as the helmsman, was blind (she had added the bit about the helmsman only in my presence), and that I did not fully perceive the extent of her distress. Possibly the reference to the helmsman's blindness was also an expression of her feeling of missing her father, who paid too little attention to her.

At any rate, the dream and the fact that I construed it as a kind of message resulted in the planning of a therapy for Lili with another therapist. She embarked on this therapy at the age of 4.

FOLLOW-UP AND CONCLUSION

Over the course of eight years I was able to keep track of Lili's development. According to what I understood on the basis of the information I received, Lili passed through nursery school without problems and is now at primary school. She has developed into a clever and intellectually precocious girl who communicates with other people almost like an adult. She is always bubbling over with ideas, and this is greatly appreciated by her friends. However, the odd report from her mother indicates that she has a pronounced narcissistic vulnerability. I also wonder whether Lili's premature adoption of a caretaker function might represent an incipient defensive character organization.

The constancy of the object representation fluctuated and fluctuates up to now. Again and again—Lili is now 9 years old—persecutory, aggressively tinged behaviour is turning up. Lili tries from time to time to coerce her mother and to force her to do something for her that Lili thinks is necessary. It is clear that she tries to get the utmost attention from her mother. The predominance of love is unstable. It seems as if there is a persistence of modes of behavior from the rapprochement crisis, intense fear of object loss, separation anxiety, and, as I mentioned above, coerciveness, demandingness, and outbursts of temper. Nevertheless, as far as I can see from the outside, Lili is a most active person, full of ideas and very assertive.

According to the first view of the concept of object constancy so beautifully clarified by McDevitt, namely, the capacity to maintain object cathexis irrespective of gratification or frustration, I would say that Lili has been able to begin a rather satisfying development. Still, with regard to the second view, namely, the resolution of the conflicts characteristic of the rapprochement subphase, Lili's state seems still to be a rather fragile one.

REFERENCES

Freud, A. (1965). *Normality and Pathology in Childhood*. New York: International Universities Press.

Galenson, E. (1984). Psychoanalytic approach to psychotic disturbances in very young children. *Hillside Journal of Clinical Psychiatry* 6:221–244.

_____ (1991). Treatment of psychological disorders of early childhood. In *Beyond the Symbiotic Orbit: Advances in Separation–Individuation Theory*—Essays in *Honor of Selma Kramer, M.D.*, ed. S. Akhtar and H. Parens, pp. 323–336. Hillsdale, NJ: The Analytic Press.

Mahler, M. S. (1967). On human symbiosis and the vicissitudes of individuation. In *The Selected Papers of Margaret S. Mahler*, vol. 2, pp. 77–98. New York: Jason Aronson, 1979.

_____ (1974). Symbiosis and individuation: the psychological birth of the human infant. In *The Selected Papers of Margaret S. Mahler*, vol. 2, pp. 149–168. New York: Jason Aronson, 1979.

Mahler, M. S., Pine, F., and Bergman, A. (1975). *The Psychological Birth of the Human Infant*. New York: Basic Books.

Winnicott, D. W. (1963). The development of the capacity for concern. In *The Maturational Processes and the Facilitating Environment*, pp. 73–82. New York: International Universities Press, 1965.

IDENTIFICATIONS ON THE WAY
TO CONSTANCY
by Anni Bergman, Ph.D.

The fourth subphase of the separation–individuation process, *on the way to object constancy*, follows the resolution of the rapprochement crisis. The way in which the rapprochement crisis is resolved is influenced by the quality of the mother–child relationship, in particular, the mother's emotional availability. While the resolution of the rapprochement crisis marks a milestone in development, achieving object constancy is an ongoing developmental life task.

SOME REFLECTIONS ON McDEVITT'S
OBSERVATIONS

John McDevitt (see Chapter 2) sees object constancy as a compromise formation, bringing it into the mainstream of psychoanalytic thinking about conflict and making it part of the structural theory about conflict and compromise formations. His major contribution consists in showing that conflict and compromise formation do not begin with the resolution of the oedipal conflict but can be traced to the progressions and regressions in development within the mother–toddler relationship. He demonstrates how this works in the case of Donna, whose mother was optimally available, and he shows in particular how Donna solved her rapprochement crisis by way of identification with the good caretaking mother as well as with the prohibitions imposed by her. In his discussion of two treatment cases with compromised object constancy, he shows furthermore that object constancy is not achieved where an early satisfactory relationship between infant and mother has been missing. This results in splitting of the object world to such an extent that the good mother does not become intrapsychically available.

Seeing object constancy as a process rather than an end point makes it comparable to reaching the depressive position in the Kleinian sense, which assumes acceptance of separateness and with that renunciation of projective identification as a major mechanism of defense. Projective identification binds subject and object together in negative interactions in which the border between the actor and the one who is acted on is not clearly defined. This is reminiscent of what we see during the rapprochement crisis, where battles between toddler and mother often can be seen as a toddler's wish to coerce the mother to provide "impossible solutions" that would confirm the toddler's still omnipotent view of the world in which separation of *I* and *you* cannot be accepted. Reaching the depressive position implies a process of mourning, which Mahler has also described as characteristic of the rapprochement subphase, in which the toddler has to come to terms with aloneness, separateness, and relative helplessness (Mahler 1966). In the thinking of Kleinians, reaching the depressive position is, like object constancy in Mahler's sense, a life task. In Kleinian thinking, there is always a danger of regression into the paranoid position, which is similar to the rapprochement crisis. Steiner describes the stages in reaching the depressive position. He says:

> A critical point in the depressive position arises when the task of relinquishing control over the object has to be faced. The earlier trend, which aims at possessing the object and denying reality, has to be reversed if the depressive position is to be worked through, and the object is to be allowed its independence. [Steiner 1992, p. 53]

Separation-individuation theory was developed out of the observations of mother–child pairs by psychoanalytically trained observers. The purpose of these observations was not just to describe behaviors but to draw inferences about the internal world of the infant and toddler. It is important to realize that the presence of the mother was an integral part of the setting because the focus of observation was on the interaction between them. Kleinian theory, on the other hand, reached its formulations about the internal world from observations in the clinical situation with both children and adults.

McDevitt explores the role of identification in the resolution of the rapprochement crisis. Identification precedes words and representational thought. It is also subject to a developmental process. For example, in the film *On the Development of the Sense of Self* we show how an infant whose mother is not optimally available identified with the mother's pattern of soothing her by rocking herself as she has been rocked by her mother (Mahler et al. 1982). A question to be investigated further is whether such early sensory-motor identifications are characteristic for infants who do not receive adequate mothering and therefore have to play mother to themselves prematurely. There are, however, observable preverbal identifications that seem to be universal. For example, babies at around 6 months of age will often try to feed Mother as they have been fed by her. Early games of role exchange take place around the beginning of rapprochement. For example, a little boy around 14 months of age plays that he is going out, leaving Mommy, and commands her to cry. Then he returns, reuniting with her joyfully. In this case he identifies with the mother who leaves, as he directs her identity with the baby who is left and cries. Thus, he makes sure that she knows how he feels when she leaves him. He teaches his mother to empathize with his grief, but also with his joy at reunion. How does this relate to Donna, who at this same age plays mother to dolls while Mother is out of the room? In McDevitt's description she becomes an exact replica of her good mother, thus holding on to her in fantasy. But where in her process of identification and internalization is the bad mother who left her? Is the little boy who plays both parts able to do so because he is not afraid that he will be rejected by his mother if he temporarily rejects her or is angry with her? Or is Donna protecting both herself and her mother if in Mother's absence she becomes the good mother of her dolls? In this way she protects both herself and her mother from having to feel sadness at being left. It seems to me that this question has special importance in Donna's case, because McDevitt found that Donna as an adult identifies with her mother to the point of identifying with her reaction formations and possibly sacrificing a creative step in her individuation.

McDevitt notes that in a study of the separation-individuation process boys developed object constancy in the same way as girls up to the middle of the rapprochement subphase. Then, he says, "[boys] began to move away both physically and psychologically from their mothers; they turned toward their fathers, toward father substitutes, and toward more masculine, phallic, aggressive activities and play." Boys resolve ambivalence and conflict by identifying with their fathers, just as girls resolve conflict by identifying with their mothers. I believe that this formulation may leave out complexities in development that relate to boys' early identification with Mother and girls' identification with Father (Benjamin 1991). It would be interesting to look further at the complexities of the resolution of the rapprochement crisis and how this process differs in boys and girls.

In an earlier paper with Maria Fahey (Bergman and Fahey 1994), we compare a boy and a girl during the separation-individuation process with particular attention to their reaction to fluctuations in Mother's emotional availability and to the fact that girls have to both dis-identify and identify with their mothers, while boys can identify with their fathers but have to dis-identify with their mothers in order to become separate and confirm their masculine identity. This complex developmental process contains an inherent conflict for the girl that is very well captured by Phyllis Tyson (1986), who says:

The little girl values being feminine, maternal, and "at one with" her objects. This sense of closeness and reciprocity in object relationships becomes part of a wished-for view of herself as her ego ideal is established. However, wishes to be "at one with" the ideally viewed mother conflict with the child's efforts to differentiate and separate from the mother, to resist the regressive dependent pull, and to establish a degree of autonomy. [p. 359]

A boy, on the other hand, risks moving away from Mother too quickly and developing pseudo-independence, neglecting the deeper longings for the mother. I will discuss the development of one of the boys in the separation-individuation study toward object constancy, as described by McDevitt, and I will discuss some of his conflicts as they revealed themselves during the follow-up study.

Identifications in the Observational Study and Follow-up of a Boy

Bobby: Early Observations

Bobby was the second son of his parents, and his mother was very concerned about his older brother. She weaned Bobby abruptly when he was 3 months old. She said that she was too busy taking her older son to nursery school, that she anticipated taking classes soon, and that therefore breast-feeding was too restrictive. As she fed him the bottle, she said that he loved it. But the baby developed a diaper rash, and mother began to look tired, harassed, and sad. All observers noted how this was in sharp contrast to the preceding week when she had been so happy and proud of her baby. As soon as Bobby fell asleep, Mother compared him unfavorably with her older child. By the time Bobby was 6 months old, he succeeded in engaging his mother, and with that, he became much more animated and lively. He also became much more active, began to crawl, and began to protest when he didn't get what he wanted. Bobby's mother reacted very positively when he began to show some primitive identificatory behaviors, such as feeding her and patting her on the back when she was patting him. He also began to imitate sounds. Yet when he looked to her for comforting, she saw it as weakness on his part, and she complained that at home he followed her around and she couldn't get away. Bobby learned early what pleased his mother and was able to come through for her. However, it was also observed that he developed a tendency to take on more than he could handle.

Bobby developed well during the differentiation and especially during the practicing subphase. He used his developing motor skills to explore the surroundings and to distance himself from his mother. She was pleased whenever he returned to her, but also frightened by the responsibility of his dependence on her. He began to notice and at times be upset by her absence from the room. By the time he was 10 months old, she enjoyed him and said that he was doing funny things all the time. He was smiling and engaging with observers and seemed to have learned well how to amuse and engage his mother. He started to play peekaboo with his mother and with his older brother. He tried to placate his older brother when his brother was angry with him. He took his first steps at 12 months, walking out of an open door. By 13 months he began to imitate words and made many sounds. At 15 months during a home visit, it was noted that he constantly had a bottle in his mouth, even though he was eating adult foods. Here one can see a conflict between his rapidly developing individuation and his need to be a baby.

During the rapprochement subphase at about 18 months, he began to go to his mother more frequently and to share his experiences with her. He said many words and began to notice his mother's absences from the room more immediately. When she went out for her weekly interviews, he began to sense the time when she was about to leave and would rush toward her with tears in his eyes and cling to her. Eventually he accepted her comings and goings, but his mood was low-keyed in her absence. By 19 months he began to explore the adjoining toddler room, and now when Mother was about to leave, he would leave first, going into the toddler room, which made the separation easier for him. He began to play more actively in her absence; cars and trucks became his favorite toys. During this time when he accepted separation from his mother better, he became more aggressive, especially toward his older brother and toward the younger children in the toddler room. He began to use the word "mine." He began to use the play telephone to talk to his absent father. Thus, during rapprochement he began to express wishes for being close to his father. At around 20 months he began to show further behaviors typical of the rapprochement crisis. He didn't want his mother to leave the room, and he began to retain his stools and urine. This mild rapprochement crisis came to a resolution fairly quickly, which may have been connected to his very rapid language development. He began to speak in sentences and began to use the personal pronoun "I." When his mother returned from a brief separation, he used words to tell her what he had done while she was away. Bobby was generally enthusiastic and played well with trucks and blocks and large, manipulative toys. He played constructively both when his mother was in the room and when she was out of the room. When she was out of the room, he engaged in fantasy play, having imaginary telephone conversations with her. At home he preferred his father's company and wanted to be with him whenever he could. He played at imitating his father in all kinds of activities, such as putting up shelves, hammering, and sawing. When Mother was out of the room, he tired more easily and was more aggressive. His sudden fatigue at this time seemed reminiscent of how he had reacted to the sudden weaning at 3 months.

A renewed rapprochement crisis was observed at around 23 months. This seemed to be connected to his mother's decision that he should not be allowed to play with his older brother when his older brother didn't want him to, and also with the father being away from home more in connection with taking a new job. It seems that being deprived of his male identification models at this time brought on the crisis, which took the form of refusing toilet training and heightened aggression in his play with other children. He developed a fear of tigers after his father had taken him to the zoo. At night he demanded that his father sit next to him and watch him until he fell asleep. Once when the father dozed off, Bobby awakened him and said, "Daddy, you're not watching." The confluence of rapprochement and early phallic issues became noticeable as Bobby became very concerned with body injury. He repeatedly looked at his toy animals and said that they had been hurt. He was distressed when he needed a Band-Aid. Exuberant moods began to be interspersed with moods of sudden whining and contrariness. He once again became more aggressive with younger children and did not like his mother to leave for her weekly interviews. He expressed curiosity about his body and became aware of his erections.

By 36 months this new crisis seemed to subside, and Bobby began to be willing to sit on the toilet. He flexed his muscles and felt powerful and pleased with himself. Once more he also seemed eager to please and was in better control of his impulses. However, when his mother started to go to work and someone else brought him to the center, he once again began to hold on to his stools and become more aggressive. When his mother brought him to the center on his third birthday, he was pleased and excited. He ran to her, talked to her, and showed her all the things he had been doing. He was in a delightful and expansive mood. He talked a lot, and he began to have a sense of humor, making fun of himself and acting like a clown. His mother was pleased with his development. He was still very strongly attached to the bottle and could not fall asleep without it. Mother expressed confidence that he would be able to give it up once he went to nursery school.

By the age of 3 Bobby seemed to have reached a high degree of object constancy, having resolved his rapprochement conflicts, which in his case had taken the form of refusing toilet training. One could speculate that withholding stools represented both an act of aggression toward his mother and also a symbolic way of holding on to her, as well a way to allay his castration fears. Withholding may be a relevant issue because Mother had been withholding toward him in his early infancy when she could not tolerate his needs for her. This may be seen as a way of doing to her what she had done to him when she withheld herself, refused to breast-feed, and could not tolerate his dependence on her. To the extent that withholding stools may have represented a way of holding on to her, it was a way that did not interfere with his autonomous functioning, and in that way it complied with her wishes that he should not need her too much. Bobby had turned toward his father and reacted with anger when his father became temporarily less available as an object of identification. Bobby was also helped by his ability to play and symbolize and communicate. The fact that at the age of 3 he was still so strongly attached to the bottle could be seen as a sign that the early deprivation he had experienced with his mother remained as a wound that had not quite healed, that the bottle had become a kind of transitional object.

Bobby: Adult Follow-Up

When Bobby was seen as a young man in the follow-up study, he was eager to participate and eventually asked for

therapy because he felt he needed some help resolving conflicts related to intimacy and to his tendency to overfill his life
with obligations. In his own words, he was "over-
individuated." He saw himself as having become preco-
ciously independent, left on his own to make all the important
choices in his life. All through school and college he had been
a brilliant student and artist. Though he had gone to college
on the West Coast and lived there for some years, he eventually returned to New York because he felt strongly connected
to the city and to his father. His parents had divorced during
his adolescence, and the mother had remarried. Bobby had
become responsible for overseeing the care of his aging father,
whose health was declining, but he was attentive to his own
needs by hiring a live-in caretaker for his father and an
assistant for himself. He experienced his role as Father's caretaker as something of a burden but was fully committed to it.

Bobby was living with a woman who had been abandoned as a child by her own mother. There was a great deal of
mutual caretaking between them, but the relationship was no
longer exciting enough, and he felt that he had to give up too
much of his own space to accommodate her. It seemed that he
wanted to be in therapy to be enabled to honor his own needs,
which he described as always being encroached on by his
many obligations. Bobby then found himself very attracted to
a woman whom he had admired for many years and who
seems to have admired him as well, but who was, for reasons
of her own, not available for a committed relationship. While
examining this new relationship to a somewhat unavailable
woman, he began to see the ways in which he and his mother
were unavailable to each other at the present time and became
aware of his longings to be closer to her.

Thus it seems that, despite what seemed to be satisfactory
resolution of rapprochement issues and satisfactory achievement of object constancy, Bobby remained vulnerable and

still carried within him the unfulfilled needs of his childhood, which had already begun early in his infancy. There remains in him an Achilles' heel, a fear of not being adequately loved and too much needed. He desires to find mutuality in his relationship with a woman. Maybe this is related to not having achieved mutuality early on with his mother because he had to work too hard to get her to be attentive to him.

In comparing Bobby with Donna, we see a boy and a girl who both achieve a high degree of object constancy but in young adulthood still have issues to resolve in relation to intimacy. Both remain very close to their parents. In looking at the early material about identification, there was a period when Bobby was described as strongly identifying with his father, just as Donna had been described as very strongly identifying with her mother. The early and more primitive identification with Mother had also been described in the observations of Bobby. However, quite early on he made a very pronounced effort to become independent and self-reliant. This could easily be seen as a response to Mother's early difficulty in dealing with him as a dependent infant. Thus, his independence was a compliance to Mother's needs and demands rather than an identification with a strong father. This compliance with Mother's wishes can also be seen as identification, because he left her as she had left him. By the time he went to college, where his independent strivings reached a peak, Mother had left the family to take care of her own needs. Bobby never expressed any anger or resentment toward Mother for having left the family, but rather admired her for taking care of herself. In college he became resident assistant in his dormitory and stressed that he did this when he was really too young and felt quite overwhelmed by the task. Thus we see in Bobby a very complicated process of identifying with both father and mother. As a young adult he longs to find a woman he can admire, feel close to, and identify with.

Identification in the Therapy
of Severely Disturbed Children

McDevitt describes two interesting cases in which object constancy was not achieved. In both cases this was due to the unavailability of a maternal object. It is not quite clear to me whether a degree of object constancy could be achieved as a result of the treatment process. At the City University Child Center we provide treatment for severely disturbed and deprived inner-city children in a therapeutic environment. The treatment is geared toward helping these children first reach object cathexis or attachment and then a degree of object constancy. We find that important aspects of the separation-individuation process are experienced in the therapy situation. Beginning identification with the therapist is often a sign that a significant connection has been made and the developmental process has been set in motion.

Felice*

When Felice came to the center she was a large, physically rubust girl with little comprehensible language. She related to others in an undifferentiated manner with no apparent anxiety. She had great difficulty attending to anyone or anything and was constantly on the go. She had little capacity for play. She was physically clumsy, and occasionally ran into highly visible objects in her path. Felice seemed unaware of her body and showed little emotional responsiveness. She often walked very close to the walls and touched up against them as if orienting herself in some way. She seemed unaware of physical danger. She walked on her toes. She had suffered from

---

*I would like to thank Felice's therapist Mrs. Nancy Siegel for providing the clinical material that illustrates the importance of identification.

chronic and severe asthma attacks about twice a month for more than a year.

When Felice was 18 months old, her father was shot on a neighboring street corner, and two of the mother's siblings died within six months of the shooting. Her mother had another baby when Felice was 3 years 3 months old. The baby's father died in a subway beating a week before the second baby's birth. At times Felice lives with her mother and the baby, but most of the time she lives with her grandparents and several other family members.

At the beginning of therapy, Felice could stay in the playroom for only a few minutes and would spend the rest of the therapy time wandering around the halls of the large building. The therapist writes:

> There was a compulsive, joyless quality about this roaming. It seems to be the result of overwhelming anxiety. She related very little to me, kept up a steady stream of bizarre talk, yet occasionally would turn and with a hand gesture encourage me to join her. She didn't know how to include me into her world, but it seemed to matter to her that I was there.

During the first few months of her therapy, Felice spent at least half of the sessions riding up and down in the elevator with her therapist. The therapist noted a significant turning point when after a few weeks of therapy Felice engaged in solo water play and then asked her if she wanted coffee. The therapist says:

> The development and elaboration of this activity alone significantly altered our sessions. It became the format in which she related to me, the single activity that allowed her to remain still for :ninutes at a time and signal an interest in and capacity for play. I joined her in savoring the coffee, and together we shared the enjoyment of drinking, pouring, and cleaning up spills.

Here we see the first sign of identification with a caring adult by way of imitation. Felice became fascinated with the therapist's book bag. For a month it had lain on the floor of the therapy room, but suddenly it became a new favorite object. Every session for two months thereafter contained some form of play with the book bag. She unpacked the bag piece by piece and savored each item. She was particularly fond of the American Express card, removed it and placed it in her doctor's kit. She became curious about pictures in the therapist's wallet and about her makeup. When she found the driver's license, she pointed to the therapist's picture and said, "Me." She began to apply makeup, smear lipstick all over her face, look in the hand mirror, and enjoy the way she looked. She accepted no substitutes for the therapist's bag and possessions. Along with this growing identification with the therapist, Felice developed pleasure in herself as a girl: she favored dresses, and wore her hair in frilly ways. She began more play with the therapist, saying "You be mommy, I baby" and "I mommy, you baby." The therapist reports: "As the relationship with me took hold, it was astonishing to see the way in which Felice's overall functioning developed. Everyone who came in contact with her noticed some aspect of her many developmental gains." Felice's language also began to develop: she spoke incessantly, often about aspects of her life, her grandfather, her peers, and her teachers. She cared about whether her words were understood or not. As her attachment to her therapist grew, Felice began to experience great pain at separation. The therapist says:

When our separations became too difficult, I started interpreting both the positive and negative sides of letting someone into her bubble. It was very painful to me to hear her cries. Yet it was rewarding to see that she could attach and also that she could make some healthy restitution of her equilibrium when given the time.

We see in this report how in spite of the severe traumas and separations in her life, Felice was able to use her therapist to form an intense attachment through the process of identification. She seemed, indeed, to be on the way to emotional object constancy.

CONCLUSION

Building on McDevitt's paper, I have attempted to elaborate the role of identification in both normal development and in the therapeutic situation. I have described the importance of identification in the treatment of a young girl who had suffered multiple trauma and was severely disturbed in her object relations and language development. I have also elaborated on the role of identification in the development of a boy who was seen both in early observational studies and adult follow-up and therapy. In his case, we see the complexities of identifications with both mother and father. I believe there is a need for further study of identification and gender development during separation-individuation.

REFERENCES

Benjamin, J. (1991). Father and daughter: identification with difference—a contribution to gender heterodoxy. *Psychoanalytic Dialogues* 1:277–300.

Bergman, A., and Fahey, M. (1994). Further inquiry into negotiations of separation-individuation conflicts: a boy and a girl respond to fluctuations in Mother's emotional availability. *Psychoanalytic Inquiry* 14:83–110.

Mahler, M. (1966). Notes on the development of basic moods: the depressive affect. In *The Selected Papers of Margaret S. Mahler*, vol. 2. New York: Jason Aronson, 1979.

Mahler, M. S., McDevitt, J., and Bergman, A. (1982). *The Development of the Sense of Self.* A film produced through the Margaret S. Mahler Research Foundation.

Steiner, J. (1992). The equilibrium between the paranoid-schizoid and the depressive positions. In *Clinical Lectures on Klein and Bion*, ed. R. Anderson, pp. 46–58. London: Tavistock/Routledge.

Tyson, P. (1986). Female psychological development. *Annual of Psychoanalysis* 14:357–373.

THE VALUE OF THE CONCEPT OF OBJECT CONSTANCY IN THE TREATMENT OF PSYCHOSOMATIC DISORDERS
by Paul L. Janssen, M.D.

On the basis of case material, John McDevitt argues convincingly in Chapter 2 the usefulness of developmental psychology's concept of object constancy in uncovering certain clinical phenomena. The thrust of McDevitt's argument is (1) that elements of object constancy are a capacity for libidinal binding, tolerance of separation, a facility to remember, and an ability to integrate positive and negative object representations; (2) that disturbances in object constancy are grounded in an inability to maintain stable libidinal object representations when the object is absent, or where object contact is otherwise frustrated, and that this difficulty stems from a developmental shortfall in the early years of life; and (3) that the process of attaining stable libidinal object representation is not complete until the end of the child's third year. Object constancy is consolidated through identification with the mother, and it is this internal maternal representation that guides a person in his or her actions.

McDevitt points to a whole range of ways in which object constancy can become disrupted. My only quibble with his thesis is that we do not so far have all the evidence we need to back it up. While the observation of mother–child interaction is of vital importance to the practical and conceptual advance of psychoanalytically oriented developmental psychology, the literature on child observation is as yet too meager to support all the ground-breaking theoretical work that is being done. Full corroboration will not come until more cases are followed through and more retrospective studies are carried out, taking in larger population groups. Which is not to deny that I and my team have found in the notion of object constancy a highly relevant parameter in appraising adult psychical health. We have been provided with an invaluable tool for measuring preoedipal disturbance and further tailoring psychoanalytic techniques to meet the needs of patients (cf. Blanck and Blanck 1974, 1979, 1986). Much of the work published in the field has been translated, leaving a clear imprint on the design of analytically oriented psychotherapy in Germany.

Another, no less powerful, pole of influence has been Kernberg's concept of the borderline personality (Kernberg 1975, 1976). Borderline patients suffer from disturbed object constancy. They are not able to integrate the positive and negative aspects of one and the same object. They cannot tolerate ambivalence; neither can they bear to be separated from objects in which they have made an initial emotional investment. German outpatient and inpatient analysts alike have incorporated Kernberg's thinking into their strategies for treating borderline individuals (Janssen 1987, 1990, Rohde-Dachser 1979).

THE GERMAN PERSPECTIVE

In Germany we in fact classify borderline disorders as a subgroup of what Fürstenau (1974) has usefully termed *structural ego disorders*. Practically speaking, structural ego disorder is said to be present where the use of interpretation to uncover conflict leads not to insight or psychical development—as is the expectation with neurotic patients—but rather triggers symptoms, psychical crisis, or patient withdrawal. In search of a therapeutic strategy for managing structural ego disorders, we turned to the developmental psychology of Margaret Mahler. The result was a refined definition of the problem; we began to speak of what we called disturbances in ego-self development during the period up until conclusion of the individuation phase. The criteria we adduced in order to diagnose this state were:

- an inability to differentiate between self and object;
- a lack of integration of libidinally and aggressively cathected self- and object representations;
- the persistence of primitive patterns of object relating;
- a desire for "fusion," accompanied by projective identification and splitting;
- the absence of a secure sense of identity or clear self-configuration;
- the somatization of object states (envy, anger), or else impulsive acting out.

This differentiated grid enabled us to make particular headway with psychosomatic patients (cf. Janssen 1987). Applying object constancy criteria to the treatment of psychosomatic disorders proved very stimulating for German analysts, especially those working in hospitals and in research. Our team was keen to ascertain the extent to which patients with chronic inflammation of the bowel could be subsumed under the borderline heading. Our own clinical experience (Janssen 1987, Janssen and Wienen (in press) suggested that intrapsychic mental and spiritual conflict—which in traditional borderline patients would be expressed as acting out—became somatized in patients with chronic inflammation of the bowel (e.g., Crohn's disease, ulcerative colitis). We decided to pursue this correlation by organizing a study using the standardized interview technique devised by Gunderson and Kolb (1981). Out of 38 Crohn's patients, 15 (39.5 percent) showed signs of borderline pathology. In the case of ulcerative colitis sufferers, the pattern was repeated in 3 out of 14 patients (21.4 percent). We were struck by the fact that these individuals did indeed demonstrate borderline personality features in the areas of social adjustment, emotional responsiveness, and interpersonal relations, but did not act out impulsively. Our provisional conclusion was that patients suffering from Crohn's disease and ulcerative colitis not only vented intrapsychic conflict in psychical mode but found an additional outlet in somatic symptoms. Borderline cases of this type could probably be classified as a subgroup within the category "patients with chronic inflammation of the bowel."

There is clearly a need for further research in this area, but it is fair to say that a proportion of patients with chronic bowel inflammation are subject to disturbances in object constancy similar to those diagnosed in other individuals with preoedipal disorders. After working with a homogeneous group of such patients, I and my team ventured the hypothesis that they constitute a group whose affective dysfunction is expressed as a "scream turned on the body" (Janssen and Wienen in press).

A Clinical Illustration from the
Psychosomatic Arena

Our work on the psychosomatic ward has also involved some—albeit less systematic—consideration of the psychodynamics of patients with more than one psychosomatic problem, and we have learned a number of interesting things that fit in well with McDevitt's hypothesis. Perhaps I might illustrate this using a brief clinical vignette.

> A 21-year-old patient presented with multiple complaints. Her hands were covered with eczema. Her bowels were upset; diarrhea continually alternated with constipation. She had a history of duodenal ulcers and suffered from occasional attacks of bronchial asthma. A striking feature of her background was the number of operations she had undergone—eleven in all. She was also obese, but it was the eczema that she herself chose to emphasize. Her hands would break out in a variety of situations. There was an allergic factor:

eczema was brought on by contact with certain types of fabric. Equally, psychical stress could be the trigger. A reaction often set in after she had spoken over the phone to her mother, or received a letter from her. The itching then reached such a degree of intensity that she scratched her hands until they were raw. The skin problem dated back to her third year.

As soon as she was admitted to our psychosomatic ward, the patient placed her sick body and itching hands on center stage. She constantly sought out the physician in charge, asking for ever more somatic examinations and treatment. She managed to get herself referred to all sorts of other hospitals, with the result that the possibility of surgery was raised on more than one occasion.

At the beginning she seemed to be quite beyond the reach of psychotherapy. She entrenched herself behind an intellectual wall, a position that left her feeling unwanted and rejected. Emptiness was the hallmark of her relations with others. Only when she was with the resident—to whom she "took" her sick body—did she ever sparkle with any kind of life. Meanwhile, she elicited considerable amounts of affect-laden countertransference from other members of the treatment team. Her endless demands for medical checks generated a particularly emotional level of debate within the staff group. The psychoanalysts were convinced that she was inaccessible to psychotherapeutic outreach. From an analytic perspective she incarnated an irreconcilable split between body and soul.

A glance at her biography reveals something about the origin of this split. She was born prematurely at 8 months and spent several weeks in an incubator. After the birth her mother nearly died. In future the mother was to fall ill whenever the patient was sent away on "health cures" to help her eczema.

Medical examinations and somatic treatment visibly instilled life into the patient; otherwise she seemed dead to the world, relating diffusely to others in an intellectualized and excessively rational manner. This prompted the hypothesis that the splitting was in fact a consequence of the medicalized and instrumentalized handling her body had received in her initial phase of life. She had become fixated on the "instrumental mother" (the incubator), and her subsequent efforts had been devoted to recovering the life-sustaining functions of that instrumental mother.

Our experience of inpatient psychoanalytic psychotherapy has taught us to adopt a phase-appropriate attitude. With structural ego disorders, initial therapeutic focus is on bodily awareness and expression. In Germany there is a strong commitment nowadays to "concentrative movement therapy." We favor such an approach as a means of first access to patients. In this particular case, the therapist centered her efforts on the patient's relationship with her body, for example, her partial lack of control over motor functions. Relaxation exercises were introduced, and together therapist and patient experimented with one-to-one interaction. The therapist then endeavored to talk the patient through the affective implications of certain hand movements, for example, taking or stroking the other person's hand as an expression of tenderness. This promoted the patient's awareness of the function of hands, and she gradually built up a very close rapport with the therapist. She learned to communicate her new-found sense of peacefulness and relaxation, going so far as to say that she felt as if she were listening to a lullaby when she heard the therapist's voice.

Body therapy also awakened a desire for nurture, manifested in the patient's developing relationships with the nursing staff. Little by little, she abandoned her instrumental and mechanistic use of her body. Before this stage was reached, more sophisticated psychotherapeutic approaches would have been to no avail. Subsequently, she proved accessible to art therapy and began to express her bodily feelings and her affects in image form. The next phase was to initiate verbal psychotherapy—and the patient indeed proved capable of articulating her desire for love and her need of a nurturing object.

This patient, along with many others like her who come to us for therapy, suffered from a particular kind of object

constancy disorder. McDevitt describes how psychotic patients, and severely disturbed individuals who have grown up
in institutions, seem somehow to come up against a dead end
in their development. They remain tied to a need-satisfying
object and are always searching for that object in their current
relationships. It was obvious in this case, however, that our
patient was not actively "recalling" an original need-
satisfying, living mother, that is, a comforting object; she was
still bound to an "instrumental mother" (the incubator),
which she persistently sought in medical treatment—even
pain-inducing treatment.

Her ego development had, we felt, been disturbed during
the primary autistic or symbiotic phase, resulting in considerable structural ego damage. Her structural shortfall involved what Adler and Buie (1979) (cf. McDevitt) refer to as a
cognitive defect. Her evocative memory had been disturbed
or overlaid by "artificial attachments." The disorder thus did
not stem from an inability to maintain a stable libidinal object
representation, as was the case in McDevitt's examples; instead, our patient remained tied to a nonmaternal object. This
meant that she was incapable of developing any kind of
autonomy vis-à-vis a love object; her actions were "fixed" as
repetitions of her relationship to an instrumental object. Further research needs to be done into the possibility that such
very early, primary disturbance might play a more frequent
part than we yet realize in the genesis of psychosomatic illness.

CONCLUSION

Out of these considerations has grown a psychoanalytically
rooted approach that enables patients, via body-oriented
work, to experience mothering, and via the linguistic or visual
representation of inner events, to learn the process of symbolization on which psychoanalytic therapy hinges. Applied to

the patient I have just been describing, this strategy gradually diminished her need for instrumental objects. Without wishing to be overprophetic, I believe that we are now firmly on the road toward some very exciting new work with psychosomatic patients, drawing on both Mahler's psychoanalytically oriented developmental psychology and the concept of object constancy.

ACKNOWLEDGMENT

The author thanks Ms. Dinah Cannell for translating his original German manuscript into this English version.

REFERENCES

Adler, G., and Buie, D. H. (1979). Aloneness and borderline psychopathology: the possible relevance of child developmental issues. *International Journal of Psycho-Analysis* 60:83–96.

Blanck, G., and Blanck R. (1974). *Ego Psychology: Theory and Practice.* New York: Columbia University Press.

———— (1979). *Ego Psychology II: Psychoanalytic Development Psychology.* New York: Columbia University Press.

Blanck, R., and Blanck, G. (1986). *Beyond Ego Psychology: Developmental Object Relations Theory.* New York: Columbia University Press.

Fürstenau, P. (1974). Die beiden Dimensionen des psychoanalytischen Umgangs mit strukturell Ich-gestörten Patienten. *Psyche* 31:197–207.

Gunderson, J. G., and Kolb, J. E. (1981). The diagnostic interview for borderline patients. *American Journal of Psychiatry* 132:896–903.

Janssen, P. L. (1987). *Psychoanalytische Therapie in der Klinik (Psychoanlaytic therapy in the hospital setting).* Stuttgart: Klett.

———— (1990). *Psychoanalytische Therapie der Borderlinestörungen.* Berlin: Springer.

Janssen, P. L., and Wienen, G. (in press). Group Analysis with ulcerative colitis and regional ileitis: the discovery of the scream. *Group Analysis.*

Kernberg, O. (1975). *Borderline Conditions and Pathological Narcissism.* New York: Jason Aronson.

———— (1976). *Object Relations Theory and Clinical Psychoanalysis.* New York: Jason Aronson.

Rohde-Dachser, C. (1979). *Das Borderline-Syndrom.* Bern: Huber.

OBJECT CONSTANCY
by Helen C. Meyers, M.D.

The concept of object constancy is of the greatest importance in child developmental studies, as well as in its clinical implications and applications for diagnostic understanding and technical treatment of both children and adults. The establishment of object constancy is essential for good object relations (internal and external) and separates the neurotic character from lower-level pathology—borderline and psychotic structure.

DEVELOPMENT

When is object constancy established? Is it established, for that matter, at one point, or is it a gradual development that may even go on throughout life? Related to that, can the object be partially constant, or is it all or nothing? Is the object either constant or fragmented? And once object constancy is established, is it definitely established, or does it fluctuate? Is it subject to regression, splitting, and disintegration not only in borderline (and psychotic) patients but in ordinary neurotics under stress? And finally, does the establishment of object constancy have to include the *working through* of ambivalence, that is, the neutralization of aggression, or does it really involve the *tolerance* of ambivalence—or are these two actually the same thing, that is, tolerance of ambivalence requiring sufficient neutralization of aggression to make it safe? Is it a matter of a quantity or a quality difference?

The concept of object constancy seems to me definite and clear: it means the establishment of a permanent or constant internal representation of object (originally the mother), which remains there, steady over time, whether the object is present or not and whether it is need fulfilling or not at any given time; it includes both good and bad images of the object, that is, both need fulfilling (= "good," loving) and frustrating and rejecting (= "bad," aggressive) aspects of the object, under the predominance of the good. It thus includes both affective (libidinal and aggressive) development and cognitive maturation, since it requires at least the attainment of self-other differentiation, the recognition and representation of a whole other or object and a whole self-representation, an ongoing affective attachment to that object and its internal representation, as well as attainment of symbolic thinking to form this internal representation, and the capacity for evocative memory to recall this representation in the absence of the external object. The optimal development of object constancy depends on interaction with an empathically perceptive, developmentally attuned, physically available and therefore safe object; it can be developed with several caretakers, but not with too many, it can survive short periods of object loss, but may be lost with long loss early in childhood.

According to Settlage (1990, 1993) object constancy is the foundation for empathy, thinking, and working through object loss, can be measured in terms of the child's tolerance for separation from the primary love object, and can be redefined at each level of development in terms of its function: (1) In preschool, it serves to cope with separation anxiety. (2) In school, it is the source of self-esteem to deal with failures in cognition and social challenges. (3) In adolescence, it provides a sense of wholeness. (4) In adulthood, it provides a dependable, unique identity.

The timing of the development of object constancy will, of course, depend on one's definition. In my definition (above) the sequence is from simple need-fulfillment requirements to attachment to the need-fulfilling object around the age of 8 months when recognition memory has been established and the need-fulfilling mother (the object of attachment) is recognized when she appears, but not recalled when she is absent (and thus unavailable for support—leading to stranger anxiety). This has been referred to by some authors as the "first" libidinal constancy (not to be confused with the later true object constancy). To me, though, this is more like perceptual constancy or permanence. This is followed at 18 months by Piaget's (1937) object permanence (or conceptual constancy), when evocative memory is established with the beginning of symbolic thinking, enabling objects (nonhuman objects) to be mentally represented and, therefore, spontaneously recalled and played with mentally. It is not, however, until toward 36 months (36 months according to Hartmann [1952], 24–36 months "on the way to object constancy" according to Mahler [1967, 1974]) that mental representations of human objects (mother), both good and bad, can be integrated into one whole representation under the dominance of the good, and object constancy is established. According to Mahler this also means that the ambivalence of the rapprochement phase has to be worked through. Another way of looking at this, though, is that if the aggressively invested object representations are too strong, or archaic, the threat to the good object representations of being overwhelmed is too great and they cannot be integrated—a protective, defensive split is maintained, such as in borderline pathology, and object constancy is not achieved.

Thus, as mentioned before, both affect development, libidinal and aggressive, as well as cognitive maturation are intrinsically involved; ambivalence, to my mind, has to be tolerated within one, whole, integrated representation, but the aggression must be manageable enough—sublimated, or neutralized, or attenuated—to maintain a whole, predominantly good, constant internal object safely—whether the external object is need-satisfying or frustrating, present or absent, at a particular time.

Derailments and Disturbances

Now, once established, the interesting question is, Can object constancy be lost again or disintegrate under stress? Obviously, if it is not established, or is only partially established, whatever is constant can easily be lost, or be subject to disintegration. But what happens to solidly established object constancy? To my way of thinking, object constancy is really more of a *capacity* to maintain constant objects than a specific object relationship—and this capacity as such, once established, does not get lost. A particular *content* of an object representation will, of course, change in development or in analysis, for better or worse, can temporarily be very aggressively or positively inverted; but that would not have to change the constancy of the internal relationship to that object. However, taking it a step further, might not even an integrated constant object, in the neurotic, temporarily split under stress in the transference in analysis, with regression to an earlier stage? What then? I do believe this would be temporary, often not complete, and fairly quickly disintegrated.

Let me give you an example: In the fourth year of analysis, in a regressed transference, a well-integrated young woman's usually well-balanced constant object relationship split wide open in relation to a particular set of interpretations, and the analyst became the controlling, abusive father, at whom she ranted and railed with intense fury. Nothing else remained. Gone was the "good," interested analyst, the longed-for supportive mother image, the therapeutic alliance—only blind rage for session after session. And yet the "good" image and positive value of the relationship were not lost, the constant object relation had not disappeared. The patient did return again and again, and after many sessions of abuse and paranoid-like accusations, this particular regressed transference fantasy was worked through with interpretation to everyone's satisfaction. We have all had many such instances, I am sure. Was this a loss of object constancy, even temporarily? Certainly the capacity for object constancy was not lost.

Of course, matters are quite different for patients (with

borderline pathology, for instance) who never fully attained object constancy, never fully were able to internalize a need-fulfilling object, never had a "good" mother to identity with, and could form neither an integrated constant object nor an integrated cohesive self-representation. These patients use a variety of internal coping mechanisms to deal with this split, this need to fill in the missing something, this fear of separation or engulfment or emptiness and they present a variety of interesting technical challenges in analysis. Let me briefly illustrate three such withdrawals from object constancy:

In one case, a very bright, talented, and effective young woman dealt with early object loss of both parents and abandonment by all relatives to a hostile foster home by isolation and distancing and an inability to depend on anyone—"there was no need for any object relations." There was no such thing as a constant object—neither foster mother nor relatives in her adolescence or later had any existence for her. In the transference she could not trust or admit to a need for the analyst. The analyst's vacations led to further cool withdrawal, with the image of the analyst as nonexisting during the separation. Like McDevitt's patient Mrs. A., she could not remember what the analyst looked like. Indeed, vacations became an interesting barometer of progress over the years. As the analytic work continued, both with interpretations and reconstructions, and a constant analytic relationship—where the analyst came and listened steadfastly, not coming too close but remaining reliable and dependable—slowly the patient admitted to a beginning sense of object relatedness. That summer when vacation time approached, the patient went into a steely rage that lasted for weeks, feeling betrayed, abandoned, and abused by the analyst. Now that she had permitted herself a glimmer of dependence, she felt the image of the "good" analyst could not be maintained during the absence. As this was worked through, several years later the patient was able to respond to the summer break with some comfort, verbalizing that for the first time she felt she could maintain an inner image of the analyst, "not perfect but good enough." Object constancy seemed to have been achieved.

In the case of Mrs. A. cited by McDevitt, we might speculate that his patient dealt with lack of object constancy with early preoedipal sexualization. With the neglect and nonresponsiveness on the part of the mother (and maybe even early sexual stimulation from the father), the patient compensated to fill the void—and soothe herself—with an autoerotic fixation or regression on both an oral and a genital level, leading to an intensification of the later oedipal conflict (as described by Roiphe and Galenson [1973] in severely traumatized children). This self need-fulfilling adaptation then led to the formation of an addictive personality both on an oral and a genital sexual level—the patient was an alcoholic and "addicted" to the relationship with the analyst, demanding that he be there for her all the time. The sexualization thus represented a continuation of a need-satisfying relationship, instead of establishing object constancy.

A third (and final) borderline patient—with a background of an absent father and a destructive, hostile, competitive mother—was unable to identify with a loving, empathic mother representation and could not develop basic trust. She dealt with this lack of object constancy by concrete clinging in the analytic relationship, with demands for physical closeness and hand-holding, but no sexualization. Her inability to separate from the hostile mother was mirrored by her inability to separate from the analyst. We must, however, be careful not to make these *direct* translations from the past to the present transference—since, particularly in lower-level pathology patients, the transference is a very distorted, reworked repetition. At any rate, her object representations were extremes of all bad and denegrated or all good and idealized images held apart by a defensive split and paranoid projections. The task of healing this split of good and bad (to even approach object

constancy) involved confrontation in the transference, interpretations of the split with its defensive origin in aggression
and deprivation, and reconstructions, as well as the use of the
sustaining, holding (though *not* physical), interpersonal "dia-
trophic relationship" (Loewald 1960), including "trans-
muting internalization" (Kohut 1977) and validation in which
both patient and analyst continued constantly and survived.

REFERENCES

Hartmann, H. (1952). The mutual influences in the development of the ego and the id. *Psychoanalytic Study of the Child* 7:9–30.

Kohut, H. (1977). *The Restoration of the Self*. New York: International Universities Press.

Loewald, H. W. (1960). On the therapeutic action of psychoanalysis. *International Journal of Psycho-Analysis* 41:16–33.

Mahler, M. S. (1967). On human symbiosis and the vicissitudes of individuation. In *The Selected Papers of Margaret S. Mahler*, vol. 2, pp. 77–98. New York: Jason Aronson, 1979.

_____ (1974). Symbiosis and individuation: the psychological birth of the human infant. In *The Selected Papers of Margaret S. Mahler*, vol. 2, pp. 149–168. New York: Jason Aronson, 1979.

Piaget, J. (1937). *The Child's Construction of Reality*, trans. M. Cook. London: Kegan Paul, 1955.

Roiphe, H., and Galenson, E. (1973). Object loss and early sexual development. *Psychoanalytic Quarterly* 42:73–90.

Settlage, C. F. (1990). Childhood to adulthood: structural change in development toward independence and autonomy. In *New Dimensions in Adult Development*, ed. R. A. Nemiroff and C. A. Colarusso, pp. 226–243. New York: Basic Books.

_____ (1993). Therapeutic process and developmental process in the restructuring of object- and self-constancy. *Journal of the American Psychoanalytic Association* 41:473–492.

4

THE DEVELOPMENT OF OBJECT CONSTANCY AND ITS DEVIATIONS

Phyllis Tyson, Ph.D.

Object relations theory is concerned with how significant perceived and felt interactions with others affect the origin, nature, and functioning of intrapsychic structures. It is central to contemporary psychoanalysis. This interest can be traced back at least as far as the ego psychologists of the 1950s. Hartmann (1952) was particularly interested in ego development, and he thought that the mother–child relationship was crucial. He wondered what it was in the early mother–child relationship that contributed to the formation of a secure, independently functioning individual. Critical of oversimplified views of a "bad" or "good" mother, he noticed that what appeared on the surface to be "good" object relations may nevertheless be a developmental handicap if the child does not learn to function independently but instead remains dependent on the mother (1952, p. 163). Hartmann concluded that ego development and object relations are correlated in complex ways and that satisfactory object relations can only be assessed in terms of ego development. He thought that by assessing the extent to which object constancy is achieved, some judgment could be made about the child's capacity to function independently. And he suggested by implication that an assessment of object constancy can lead to a reliable conclusion about ego development.

Unfortunately, Hartmann did little to define or elaborate what he meant by object constancy. However, the concept had immediate appeal and quickly found its place in the psychoanalytic lexicon, sometimes with the term *libidinal* attached to it, sometimes not. Yet, like so many of our terms, the same term has been used by several theorists but in different ways and referring to different phenomena. This lack of consistency makes a potentially useful concept confusing. The purpose of this chapter is, first, to clarify this concept and, second, to demonstrate the way in which the concept can be useful in our diagnostic understanding of children and, by inference, adults.[1]

The concept of object constancy has been used in several different ways by various theorists. I shall consider four major ones, that is, the formulations of Spitz, Anna Freud, Piaget, and Mahler.

FOUR DIFFERENT VIEWS

Spitz

In studying the intertwining of object relations, affects, and ego development, Spitz (1959) referred to the developmental

---

[1]In his early work Freud used the term *das Ich* (translated as "ego") to refer to an experiential sense of one's self. When he proposed his structural hypothesis, he added that the ego could also be thought of as "a coherent organization of mental processes" consisting of all those functions that regulate the drives and adapt to reality (1923, p. 17). In other words, two levels of abstraction are implied: an experiential level, which leads to the formation of self- and object representations, and a nonexperiential level, which functions as an organizer, synthesizer, and regulator of the personality. Throughout this paper, when I refer to ego development, I imply both meanings, an experiential self, the continued integrity of which is due to the functioning of the nonexperiential ego (see Tyson and Tyson 1990 for further elaboration).

achievement of the mother becoming the constant libidinal object. He noticed that during the first several months of life, the infant responds with a smile and pleasure to the approach of almost any human being. Even the mother's nurturing and soothing functions can be assumed by a substitute caregiver at times. But by about 8 months this changes; a firm attachment to the mother[2] can be observed, and she is consistently preferred above all others. Strangers or substitutes, instead of being freely accepted, may be greeted with distress as the infant searches for the safety of the mother. In his various writings, Spitz implies that the mother as the constant libidinal object has an auxiliary ego function in that she assures the infant's sense of safety. As the "preferred above others person," the infant looks to the mother for affective cues before exploring new territory or new toys. A frown or look of distress from the mother causes the infant to pull back, to cling to the mother in distress. Given an approving nod or smile, the infant explores happily. This phenomenon, known more recently as social referencing, has been more extensively studied by Emde (1980), a late collaborator of Spitz.

Anna Freud

Anna Freud (1963, 1965) traced a line of development of object relations. Coming primarily from a position of psychoanalytic drive theory, she referred to libidinal investment, that is, to the child's capacity to maintain interest in, attachment to, and affection for the mother whether she frustrates or satisfies the child's wishes. As Anna Freud used the concept, before object constancy, the child turns toward the object at the time of need, for example, when experiencing hunger, but then withdraws attention once the need has

---

[2]Throughout this paper I shall use the term *mother* to refer to the primary caregiver, recognizing that this could be mother, father, other, or a composite of any or all.

been satisfied. The child also withdraws attention from the unsatisfactory or unsatisfying object. After object constancy becomes established (which Anna Freud thought occurred in the latter half of the first year, that is, once a secure attachment had been made), the mother keeps her special place for the child whether she satisfies or frustrates (1968, p. 506). In elaborating on this notion of object constancy, Solnit and Neubauer (1986) emphasize how important it is for us to recognize the strength of the mother–child bond. Once this developmental achievement is accomplished, attachment remains constant even if the relationship is not a particularly healthy one. Indeed, this bond can endure despite sometimes life-threatening, abusive, and destructive pathological situations. It is imperative to keep in mind the nature of this constant attachment if we are to intervene meaningfully in situations of neglect and abuse.

Piaget

Working within the context of cognitive psychology, Piaget focused on the steps leading from perception of an object to evocative memory. He employed the term *permanence* for the achievement of an object concept and reported that by 18 months the small child demonstrates that he can maintain an inner image of the object that exists independent of his perception of it. Fraiberg (1969) points out that the term *constancy*, as used in general psychology, was an important aspect of Piaget's concept. This constancy referred to an object that "preserves its essential character despite variations introduced into the situation surrounding it" (Werner 1957, p. 108). For Piaget, then, by 18 months the child can maintain and recall a stable, objective, cognitive mental representation of the mother (or other) that preserves its essential character despite variations in the surrounding situation.

Mahler

Mahler also formulated a developmental line of object relations, and for her the concept of object constancy is also fundamental. However, whereas the object constancy discussed by both Anna Freud and Spitz involved developmental milestones accomplished between 6 and 10 months in the normal developing infant, and Piaget's concept referred to a cognitive achievement of the 18-month-old, Mahler's is a more sophisticated and complicated concept. She stresses not the attachment, as does Spitz, nor the drive-determined tenacity of the attachment, as does Anna Freud, nor simply the endurance of the cognitive representation, as does Piaget. Rather, she concentrates on the role of object relations in psychic structure formation. Focusing on internalization, or the mental representation of the mother and the way in which this representation functions, Mahler says, "At times of mother's absence the representation continues to provide sustenance, comfort, and love" (1968, p. 222). In other words, there is an enduring inner sense of mother's loving presence, even at times when she is not physically present. This developmental achievement is accomplished first by forming a firm attachment to the mother as the constant libidinal object (Spitz). We might call this the first level of object constancy. Then the mother remains the constant object irrespective of gratification or frustration that is, the drive aspect stressed by Anna Freud. Perhaps we can call this the second level of object constancy. Later, by 18 to 22 months, a stable, integrated cognitive representation coalesces as Piaget and other cognitive psychologists have studied it. We can call this the third level of object constancy. Finally, some resolution of anal-phase struggles is required, so that affective components can be integrated. That is, the loving and hating feelings toward the object, the views of the object as alternately "good" and "bad," can be integrated (McDevitt 1975, 1979). With an integrated, durable inner sense of the mother to which the child can cling when frustrated or angry, the child is able to derive progressively more comfort from the internal image. With an enduring inner sense of a loving mother, the child is able increasingly to function more adequately separate from the mother. Object relating can then progress to more sophisticated levels.

Clearly there is a significant discrepancy between the concepts of Spitz, Anna Freud, Piaget, and Mahler. Whereas Spitz and Anna Freud describe optimal developmental achievements for the infant in the first year, laying excessive stress on these early markers (or lack of their achievement) may give us unreliable clues about later ego functioning. To be sure, if the infant is unable to reach these early stages in object relating, his ego development is likely to be affected.

However, Mahler's stress on the object representation also has disadvantages. Students sometimes confuse cognitive and libidinal aspects and assume that during emotional storms it is the integrated representation that becomes lost, disrupted, or split apart. This does not fit with clinical experience. The child may feel the loss of the loving connection at times of heightened hostility, leading to a state of feeling bereft, abandoned. However, under most circumstances, by 20 to 24 months, a normally intelligent child is nevertheless able to maintain a mental representation of the mother that preserves her essential character despite these affective fluctuations or despite variations in the physical surroundings. It may be that by emphasizing representational concepts, we have fostered a blurring of cognitive and structural concepts.

Rather than stress the nature of the representation, I would like to concentrate on the nature of ego functioning. I return to Hartmann's question, What is it that contributes to the child eventually being capable of independent functioning? I will use the capacity for affective self-regulation as a central characteristic by which to judge the capacity for independent functioning.

Affects are chiefly associated with pleasure, or with danger. Danger can be real, in the external world, or danger can be intrapsychic, that is, related to conflict and fears of consequence lest forbidden impulses find expression. Affects can function in two ways in psychic life. When especially intense, or when self-regulatory functions are weak or immature, affects can disrupt and disorganize self-regulation. If instead, before it reaches this intensity, the child (or adult) can perceive the affect, identify the danger (external or internal), and adjust behavior accordingly, with the help of defense and compromise, we can say the affect has served a signal function. The child's capacity to use affects as signals is not an automatic characteristic of affect, but rather a developmental achievement.

What is it in the mother–child relationship that fosters the development of the child's capacity for affective self-regulation independent of the mother's immediate availability? This question is an intriguing one because, as clinicians are quite aware, there are individuals who are incapable of self-regulation despite a constant attachment and despite an enduring representation of the mother.

Infant researchers (e.g., Stern 1974, 1985) have made us aware that as early as 4 months, important self-regulating behaviors emerge within mother–infant exchanges when the mother is functioning optimally as a soother, comforter, and regulator. The developmental conflicts of the anal-rapprochement phase, as more expectations are placed on the young child, typically arouse intense affective states. Consequently, greater demands are made on the as yet immature self-regulatory functions. Without timely intervention and the mother's comforting, regulating, and reorganizing responses, the toddler easily feels desperately helpless and defensively angry. There is often a fine line, not always distinguishable by the observer, between overwhelming anxiety and rage. Anger is easily projected, and instead of an object of safety, at these times the mother may be viewed as a persecutor; the accompanying anxiety easily disrupts ego functioning. This creates a state of helplessness and a sense of loss of the libidinal connection with the mother, a situation so often seen when a young child is in the midst of a temper tantrum (Yorke and Wiseberg 1976).

If the mother herself is not overly distressed by the toddler's demands or distress, she can respond to this display of feelings with a balance between some tolerance of the child's impulse, on the one hand, and appropriate, consistent expectations of compliance, on the other, with some organizing responses that help the child regain control and equilibrium. In this way she prevents the accompanying affects from reaching proportions that undermine ego functioning and self-regulation. Such a regulating balance reduces distress, encourages the building of frustration tolerance (because she nevertheless expects compliance within the child's capacity), and it encourages self-coping mechanisms. The mother's regulating balance also reassures the toddler of the enduring nature of the mother's loving availability. This contributes to the child's developing an increasing capacity for affective control. If the mother is successful in her role as an auxiliary ego, the child's identification with her would ultimately include identification with her anticipation of and regulatory responses to danger. Regulatory functioning can then be increasingly available to the child as an ego function. In other words, if the child can reach the level of libidinal object constancy as defined by Mahler, this identification with her regulatory response to danger is internalized (Tyson 1988, see also Pine 1971, Settlage 1980). Consequently, even if object relations do not appear to be "good enough," a more reliable measure of their adequacy would be the child's capacity for affect regulation.

With regard to psychopathology, questions about causative factors arise when children are unable to reach an adequate or age-appropriate level of affect regulation despite what appears to be a good mother–child relationship. In attempts to understand such children (and adults), I have reconsidered Winnicott's idea of the use of the object. Winnicott differentiates object relating and object use. As he uses the concepts, he says that in object relating there is not a clear differentiation between object and subject; in other words, the child's perception of the object is heavily influenced by the child's own projections. Object use, by contrast, involves the child's perceiving the nature and behavior of the object, free of his own projections. If the object is to be used, Winnicott says, it must "be real in the sense of being part of shared reality, not a bundle of projections" (1969, p. 88). That is, the parent must survive the child's projections. Said another way, the caregiver must not feel threatened and frightened of the child's emotions and not be stimulated or manipulated to respond threateningly or frighteningly in kind to the child. Instead, the caregiver must feel and be able to convey that a sense of continuing safety prevails in spite of the child's affective storm. In other words, the child may have murderous fantasies and erupt in rage, but the mother must reassure the child that his angry, murderous thoughts will not frighten, infuriate, hurt, or kill her. If she can tolerate these affects, indeed, remain steady and strong in the face of them and not be manipulated to give in or retaliate, but intervene in a timely way, the child will not be overwhelmed by these feelings. Furthermore, the child will then be able to discover that the mother is different from his projections. If the object can "survive" the child's attacks (which in this context, Winnicott explains, means "not retaliate"), the child can begin to recognize the object as an entity in its own right. The child will then have the opportunity to "use" the object, to learn from the object that there are adaptive ways of handling these emotions. They need not be totally stifled, experienced as destructive, or experienced as disrupting ego functioning; they can aid adaptation. In this way the child also learns to take responsibility for his actions and feelings.

Rather than this optimal response, the object often becomes distressed or enraged by the child's behavior. In cases where the mother cannot tolerate the child's affective outbursts, and either abandons or retaliates in some way (identifying with the child's projections and becoming a frightening attacker), then she ceases to function as an auxiliary ego, maintaining a feeling of safety. The object then cannot be "used," and so varieties of sadomasochistic, manipulative, or other maladaptive solutions are sought.

By way of illustration, I like to use the example of spilled milk. The child spills the milk. Mother (or Father) may say, "Oh, accidents happen. Here's a sponge, I'll help you clean it up." Affects are not magnified out of proportion, but the child also learns to take responsibility for her actions—she has to clean it up, and in so doing, learns adaptive ways of rectifying mistakes.

Another parent may perceive the spilled milk as yet another example of her inept child, or she may even perceive the accident as an attack in some way. She may then see the incident as another way in which motherhood is, for her, a masochistic exercise (see Blum 1976). So she shouts at the child, telling her in one way or another what a bad child she is, and sends her to her room. That way the child will be out of the way while she, mother as Cinderella, has to clean up the mess. The child may feel overwhelmed with emotion, feel like a bad, destructive child, and also feel enraged at the mother who becomes an attacker. The child is not helped to take responsibility, to find adaptive ways of handling emotions, or to find ways of regulating emotions. Instead, she and her mother go through cycle after cycle of sadomasochistic, dysfunctional interactions.

CLINICAL ILLUSTRATIONS

Allen

Allen's parents sought consultation when Allen was 3 years 9 months old because of his erratic behavior. He would swing from being a sweet, amicable, shy child to being impulsive, angry, bossy, and argumentative. In this mood he would often attack other children. Once, after hitting another child, he was told by the teacher that he was a bad boy. From that moment, Allen declared that Allen was dead and instead he was a bear, a cuddly, furry, sweet baby bear. He cried when he looked in the mirror to discover otherwise and erupted in fury when one of his parents called him Allen.

When they brought him for consultation, Allen's mother was herself quite distraught by Allen's anxiety and vulnerability and extreme reactions to what seemed like ordinary, everyday types of incidents. I will not elaborate Allen's treatment, but I want to indicate that in addition to seeing Allen, I also saw his mother, a very anxious, controlling woman. Working with her was often difficult, as she would become tearful thinking about what might be wrong with her child. At one point she tearfully described a painful confrontation of angry boy–angry mother, following which Allen hid under his bedcovers, frightened to look at or respond to anybody; his mother collapsed in tears on observing his behavior and sent his father in to cope with him. Thinking of Winnicott's idea of use of the object, I thought about how unavailable Allen's mother was to him—it seemed almost as if he had to be emotionally strong to take care of his mother. As long as he was not overly anxious or overly enraged, they had a close relationship. But she tended to become extremely anxious whenever he became enraged, and at those times she either attacked or withdrew. Both of these responses made her seem to be what Allen feared most, an attacker, or a mother who would abandon him.

If the child is to overcome his helplessness and use his affects adaptively, he must first experience the mother as responsive to his affects, but stable herself, and her behavior not altered by his affective storms. He can then begin to use the mother's regulating, safety-keeping functions to quiet his emotional storms, to calm his anxiety. Internalization and identification with this constant libidinal object leads to internally available regulating and safety-keeping responses. Successful internalization ensures that the child has significant inner resources for independent affect management. Once these comforting, regulating functions become available as stable internal resources, which I propose accompanies the loving functions of libidinal object constancy (Mahler et al. 1975), the object's function of responding to affective signals by regulating and organizing activities becomes part of the child's self-regulation. Gradually the child is able to recognize his own affective states, to utilize them as signals, to limit them to small proportions, and to respond with his own organizing, regulating, protecting, and adaptive activities. It is in this way that the capacity to use affects as signals to organize ego functioning effectively depends on successful use of and identification with the object.

To move this discussion beyond the level of theoretical abstraction, I turn to some other clinical examples.

Susie

Susie's mother brought her for treatment at the age of 3 years 6 months because of her oppositional and aggressive behavior. She was clingy, yet she struggled with her mother over everything—she was furious to discover, for example, that her mother had two pillows while she had only one. She had tenuous control over all bodily functions and was enuretic, slept poorly, and frequently woke with nightmares. She sucked her thumb, clung to her blanket, and was fearful of monsters.

The diagnostic evaluation gave the impression of a little girl easily overwhelmed with anxiety. She was stubborn, manipulative, domineering, prone to sadistic teasing and mimicry, and when these meager attempts to control the outside world failed, she collapsed into angry, anxious sobs. In treatment this little girl was controlling, provocative, and slow to trust, but the greatest task was managing her enormous anxiety. She frequently had a worried, anxious look on her face, dark circles under her eyes, and she collapsed into tears at the slightest hint of not getting what she wanted, not being in total control.

On her better days, Susie would attempt to divide play material such as puppets between us, but shortly, one by one, she would take them all for herself, saying she thought I had everything and she had nothing. She frequently played a mother and baby game, and anxious worries about her mother emerged. Pretending to be the mother, she first abandoned the baby, next killed the baby, then replaced the baby with another, saying "See, Baby, you're bad, horrible, and mean, and now I have a new baby I like better."

On some days Susie was not able to displace her anxieties in fantasy. These days often began with an unpleasant mother–child interaction, and I would be greeted with a distraught child who would run to my office and hide under a chair, looking fearfully at me. On one such occasion, a day after Susie had played the mother-doesn't-want-baby game, she would not let her mother leave. Sitting tearfully on her mother's lap, she dug her fingernails into her mother's hands, saying "Mommy, I hate you, I wish you were dead." With that her mother got up to leave, but Susie clung, crying, "Mommy don't go, I know you'll never come back!" Sometimes Susie could not distinguish me from her frightening inner world and perceived me as a monster. For example, one day she ran from the waiting room, terror written across her face. "Don't touch me! Get away from me you mean, horrible, naughty little girl!" She tried to attack me, and at my restrictions broke into screaming sobs and crawled under the chair. It was only quite some time later that she crawled out, sucking her thumb, and accepted my attempt at regulation, an offer to read a story.

Johnny

Johnny was 4 years 6 months old when his parents sought consultation. His developmental history is filled with traumas: these included the death of his mother when he was 16 months; a short placement in foster care; attempts by his depressed father to care for him; multiple housekeepers; and finally care from a structured but rigid and controlling step-mother. She immediately responded to the needs of the almost mute and non-toilet-trained boy, whose behavior and life seemed chaotic.

While this picture of trauma and neglect left certain remnants, diagnostic evaluation showed ample evidence of inner conflict. But Johnny, in contrast to Susie and Allen, was not overwhelmed by the associated affect, so he attempted to make internal compromises in response to conflict. He was prone to feelings of self-criticism as well of being critical of others, and feelings of guilt and low self-esteem following episodes of expression of angry feelings.

I will present a brief example from Johnny's treatment as an example of this boy's capacity for self-regulation. Having worked through to some extent Johnny's tendency toward an extremely self-critical attitude, a bossy perfectionistic mood came to dominate our work. Johnny now felt I could do nothing right. He brought in a toy boat and pretended that his family and my family went on a trip. He pretended the dad was making dinner, and since I could make my voice a low one, I had to pretend to be the dad and to announce dinner. I made a mistake in that I did not follow his words exactly, and Johnny responded in fury, "No, stupid!" I apologized, commenting on his troubling mad feelings, which got so big when I was not perfect. "Well, you're wrong and I'm right," he said. Returning to the fantasy game, he threw the doll representing me overboard to be eaten by the whale. He then had to go to the bathroom, and on returning he couldn't remember what we had been doing. I commented on his withdrawal and repression, saying he must have been very worried about feeling so mad. The following day I again displeased him, and he yelled, "Why can't you do it right? Don't you ever listen to me?" I again commented on his "big" anger when I am not perfect. With a sheepish smile he went to the window and, hiding behind the curtain, asked if I could see him. He told me a dream. "I was mad at you. We were here; I threw you out the window. At first you held on with your fingers, but then you fell, hit your head on the sidewalk, and you were dead." I asked how he felt in the dream. "Really mad at you." I commented on how scary his angry feelings were, better to have them in a dream.

DISCUSSION

Do these clinical examples shed any light on the nature of object constancy? Perhaps we can use them first to highlight the differences among the various definitions. It is clear that both Allen and Susie have strong attachments to their mothers; Mother, for both, is the libidinal object. This attachment to the mother survives whether or not their wishes are gratified. Both also have an integrated cognitive representation of the mother that remains stable in spite of emotional storms. I conclude therefore that both have reached the level of object constancy described by Spitz and Anna Freud, and both have reached the cognitive level described by Piaget. However, rather than showing evidence of being able to function separately from the mother in any kind of adaptive manner, suggesting the level of object constancy described by Mahler, both demonstrate a precarious stability in their ego functioning, with infantile narcissism and preoedipal impairment of self- and object constancy dominating the clinical picture. Their preoccupation with issues related to omnipotent demands for control, and their fears of being controlled by a frightening, angry object, suggest a lack of basic trust. Instead of a consistently loving inner presence, these children appear to have a consistent internal frightening and attacking object. This suggests a failure to tolerate ambivalence and a failure at finding some balance between the libidinal and aggressive forces within their personalities.

To Susie, neither intimacy nor separation was acceptable, for she had not found in either parent an object she could trust and use, in Winnicott's sense. Instead, Susie experienced constant tension in her environment. In addition, Susie's parents seemed unable to assist her with her distress, a quality she brought to the transference. When Susie was very upset, she would crawl under the chair in her collapsed state of tears and isolate herself, unable to accept my offers to comfort her. Initially at those times it seemed all I could do was to provide shelter. Eventually Susie would accept a story. Interestingly, as treatment progressed, Susie internalized this soothing function of mine and began to ask her mother for a story at times of distress, something the mother had not done before.

Allen's pathology also suggests early roots. While he struggled with internalized conflict that took a rather primitive concrete form, the transference indicated that he also was unable to find in his mother an object he could "use" to help him regulate his affective state.

However, sometimes we have to question—inadequate mother, or inadequate baby? From what I could gather of his early history, Allen seems to have been a hypersensitive and distress-prone infant, which may have easily interfered with his being able to experience his mother's loving attachment to him and with his ability to derive comfort from her efforts.

Being unable to comfort her child undermined his mother's confidence in her mothering skills, and the unreliable nature of his developmental progress made her increasingly anxious. Being so frightened about what was wrong with her child and insecure about how to help him forced the mother to abandon him when she was most needed, as, for example, when she collapsed in a state of anxiety in observing his regressed state. She could not then be available to be "used" by him. Rather, a demand was inadvertently placed on Allen, that he had to recover from his distressed state in order to take care of his mother.

Johnny presents a very different picture. Psychoanalytic theory suggests that a consistent, constant caretaker is essential to healthy psychological development. Consequently, we should not expect the high level of psychic functioning Johnny demonstrated, given his early history. By the time he was 3 years old, he had lost at least four caretakers, and although his father tried to be available, in reality he spent little time with the baby. However, it could be that, in contrast to Susie and Allen, Johnny was able to cope with his horrendous beginning because for him perhaps the environment was not an overly anxious one in the first year, when his father was a consistent figure. Next, when she arrived, his stepmother was not frightened or overwhelmed by the regressed child nor intimidated by the angry child. She was able to take control of the situation and to bring order and consistency into his life. In spite of his protests to the contrary, she was also able to insist on compliance. She therefore provided for Johnny an object to be used. Demonstrating the incredible resiliency of the human infant, Johnny was also able to respond and to identify with her organizing, safety-keeping functions. Because he was able to organize, stimuli were not overwhelming. The ability to organize leads to anticipation, and so Johnny could use his anxiety as a signal to defend and adapt, such as the time he left the treatment room instead of erupting when angry with me, or restricted his murderous rage to his dream.

REFERENCES

Blum, H. P. (1976). Masochism, the ego ideal, and the psychology of women. *Journal of the American Psychoanalytic Association*, 24(Suppl):157–191.

Emde, R. N. (1980). Emotional availability: a reciprocal reward system for infants and parents with implications for prevention of psychosocial disorders. In *Parent–Infant Relationships*, ed. P. M. Taylor, pp. 87–115. Orlando, FL: Grune & Stratton.

Fraiberg G. S. (1969). Object constancy and mental representation. *Psychoanalytic Study of the Child* 24:9–47. New York: International Universities Press.

Freud, A. (1963). The concept of developmental lines. *Psychoanalytic Study of the Child* 18:245–265. New York: International Universities Press.

—— (1965). Normality and pathology in childhood: assessments of development. In *The Writings of Anna Freud*, vol. 6. New York: International Universities Press.

—— (1968). Panel discussion. *International Journal of Psycho-Analysis* 49:506–512.

Freud, S. (1923). The ego and the id. *Standard Edition* 19:3–66.

Hartmann, H. (1952). The mutual influences in the development of ego and id. In *Essays on Ego Psychology*, pp. 155–182. New York: International Universities Press, 1964.

Mahler, M. S., and Furer, M. (1968). *On Human Symbiosis and the Vicissitudes of Individuation*, vol. 1, *Infantile Psychosis*. New York: International Universities Press.

Mahler, M. S., Pine, F., and Bergman, A. (1975). *The Psychological Birth of the Human Infant— Symbiosis and Individuation*. London: Hutchinson.

McDevitt, J. B. (1975). Separation-individuation and object constancy. *Journal of the American Psychoanalytic Association* 27:327–343.

—— (1979). The role of internalization in the development of object relations during the separation-individuation phase. *Journal of the American Psychoanalytic Association* 27:327–343.

Pine, F. (1971). On the separation process: universal trends and individual differences. In *Separation-Individuation: Essays in Honor of Margaret S. Mahler*, ed. J. B. McDevitt and C. F. Settlage. New York: International Universities Press.

Settlage, C. F. (1980). The psychoanalytic theory and understanding of psychic development during the second and third years of life. In *The Course of Life*, vol. 1. *Infancy and Early Childhood*, ed. S. I. Greenspan and G. H. Pollock, pp. 523–539. Washington DC: DHHS.

Solnit, A. J., and Neubauer, P. B. (1986). Object constancy and early triadic relationships. *Journal of the American Academy of Child Psychiatry* 25:23–29.

Spitz, R. A. (1959). *A Genetic Field Theory of Ego Formation: Its Implications for Pathology*. New York: International Universities Press.

Stern, D. N. (1974). The goal and structure of mother–infant play. *Journal of the American Academy of Child Psychiatry* 13:402–421.

———— (1985). *The Interpersonal World of the Infant*. New York: Basic Books.

Tyson, P. (1988). Psychic structure formation: the complementary roles of affects, drives, object relations, and conflict. *Journal of the American Psychoanalytic Association*, 36(suppl):73–98.

Tyson, P., and Tyson, R. L. (1990). *Psychoanalytic Theories of Development: An Integration*. New York: International Universities Press.

Werner, H. (1957). *Comparative Psychology of Mental Development*. New York: International Universities Press.

Winnicott, D. W. (1969). The use of an object. *International Journal of Psycho-Analysis* 50:711–716.

Yorke, C., and Wiseberg, S. (1976). A developmental view of anxiety. *Psychoanalytic Study of the Child* 31:107–135. New Haven, CT: Yale University Press.

5

WINNICOTT'S NOTION OF THE USE OF AN OBJECT

Discussion of Phyllis Tyson's Chapter "The Development of Object Constancy and Its Deviations"

Lore Schacht, M.D.

In Chapter 7 Phyllis Tyson poses the following very interesting question: What is it in the mother–child relationship that promotes the development of the capacity for self-regulation so that the child is not overwhelmed by the intensity of its affects, whether or not the mother is present? Tyson also takes up a concept of Winnicott's with which I have concerned myself for many years, and which I previously took as the starting point for the development of some further ideas (Schacht 1972), that is, why many children are unable to use the signal function. Tyson's understanding of this Winnicottian concept—or rather aspects of it—differ from my own, and in attempting to clarify the theoretical differences I hope to help formulate a new perspective.

LINKING HARTMANN AND WINNICOTT

Tyson sees a link between Hartmann's (1952) concept of object constancy and Winnicott's (1969) "use of the object,"

which, as we know, constitutes an end point in his considerations on the transitional object. In fact, both concepts crys-
tallized in 1951, the year that Hartmann first used the term
object constancy in an address to the Amsterdam International
Congress and Winnicott reported to the British Psychoanalytical Society on "transitional objects and transitional phenomena" (Winnicott had delivered his paper "The use of an
Object" to the New York Psychoanalytical Society in 1968).
And this link adds a new dimension to our thinking about the
origin of concepts. Kris used the phrase "new consideration
for the environment" in 1950. Hartmann said in his paper that
in the approach to the problem of the child's interaction with
objects, spoiling, and frustration, he had attached particular
importance to the study of the reality factor and to increasingly specific situations in the life of the child. He was
thinking of the integration of data from analytical reconstruction with data obtained from systematic—and not just occa-
sional—observation of children. My intention in now briefly
quoting the passage in which Hartmann speaks for the first
time of object constancy is to emphasize certain formulations
as the basis for a comparison between Hartmann and Winnicott:

> Ego development and object relationship are correlated in
> more complex ways than some recent works would let us
> believe . . . . We do not know much about corrections of very
> early unsatisfactory situations through later maturational pro-
> cesses. It might also be that not only can "poor" early object
> relations be something made up for by later ego development;
> but also that so-called "good" object relations may become a
> developmental handicap—probably, I should think, if and in
> so far as the child has not succeeded in utilizing them for the
> strengthening of his ego. [1952, p. 15]

I should like to point out that Winnicott thus does not actually
speak of not "succeeding in using the object," as Tyson

writes, but of "not succeeding in utilizing" good object relations.

Extreme care in the handling of formulations seems to me to be absolutely essential here, because, in a field characterized by closely related and even overlapping conceptions, it can help us to distinguish and identify firmly the contributions of different psychoanalytic authors. It is perhaps interesting to note that, on February 5, 1968, well over six months before the paper he presented in New York in that year, Winnicott wrote a two-page contribution entitled "The Use of the Word 'Use.'" He had begun to lay claim to the word *use*.

I should here like to quote a formulation from Winnicott's 1951 paper "Transitional Objects and Transitional Phenomena" because it is bears such a fascinating resemblance to the above quotation from Hartmann:

> But the term transitional object, according to my suggestion, gives room for the process of becoming able to accept difference and similarity. I think there is use for a term for the root of symbolism in time, a term that describes the infant's journey from the purely subjective to objectivity; and it seems to me that the transitional object (piece of blanket, etc.) is what we see of this journey of progress towards experiencing. [pp. 233–234]

Both concepts, Hartmann's object constancy and Winnicott's transitional object, were consigned to the psychoanalytic world in the same year, positively entrusted to the metaphors of "way" and "journey." They were both espoused enthusiastically by that world and, as the different psychoanalytic schools delved further into them, enriched with a plethora of new applications and definitions. Both concepts have now surely been accepted as among the most fundamental innovations to the theoretical edifice of psychoanalysis. Hartmann does not seem ever to have made any attempt to further clarify or deepen the concept of object constancy. In complete contrast, Winnicott spent the next two decades reflecting on and modifying his idea of the transitional object and the "journey of progress towards experiencing." He ultimately passed beyond the boundaries of psychoanalysis into the field of imaginative thought, that of cultural life and human play.

While reading the literature on object constancy in preparing this chapter, I was surprised to note the absence of any mention of the integrative function of the transitional object, which I consider it serves on the way to object constancy. I thought it strange not to find any discussion in this connection of the transitional object as the first not-me possession, the intermediate area between the subjective and that which is objectively perceived. Since Winnicott we have known that the transitional object, the first not-me possession, assumes importance for the baby when anxiety arises before going to sleep or prior to separations. Its characteristics were already described by Winnicott in 1951 so graphically that it is easy to conclude that, if a child is able to use or grasp the transitional object or invest it with life, if it can allow itself to trust the mother figure, then that child has set out on the path that leads, or may lead, to object constancy. Following Winnicott, we may take it that the use of a transitional object confirms that such a path has been embarked on.

Tyson asks the important question of what it is in the mother–child relationship that contributes to the ego's ability to function independently. In so doing, she takes the capacity for self-regulation of affect to be a central criterion of the capacity for independent functioning. What, she goes on to ask, contributes to the child's ability to cope with the intensity of its affects by self-regulation even though the mother is inaccessible or unavailable? She quotes authors, including observers of babies such as Stern (1985), who have pointed out that self-regulating behaviors already occur within the exchanges between mother and child by about the fourth month of life, provided that the mother is a comforting, calming, and regulating figure.

As a child psychiatrist with particular experience of babies and their mothers and as a psychoanalyst, Winnicott had already suggested in 1951 that the pattern of transitional phenomena first becomes evident between 4 to 6 and 8 to 12 months. He added that it was not, of course, that the object had transitional character but that the object was indicative of a transition in the child from a state of being merged with the mother to a state of being in relation to the mother as something outside and separate. Above all, Winnicott stresses the normality of transitional phenomena. However, he also considers what happens if the child cannot cope with the separation from the mother—as is possible if the mother's behavior fails to match the child's needs. For example, if the mother stays away for a period of time that is no longer tolerable, the transitional object may become meaningless. Winnicott holds that the transitional object is not an internal object, a mental concept, but that it can be used by the child indirectly, by keeping the internal object alive. It is therefore neither an internal object nor an external object. While never under magical control like an internal object, it is also not beyond the subject's control like the real mother. It thus seems to me that Winnicott's observations are borne out by authors such as Stern.

"Of the transitional object," wrote Winnicott, "it can be said that it is a matter of agreement between us and the baby that we will never ask the question: 'Did you conceive of this or was it presented to you from without?'" (1951, pp. 239–240). He insisted that the question was not to be formulated, adding that his contribution was to ask for a paradox to be accepted and tolerated and respected, and for it not to be resolved. Winnicott thus conceded an area of freedom for the unpredictable, the indeterminable, and the spontaneous in the development of the child.

For our purposes, the following are the most important of the special qualities of the relationship between the infant and the transitional object:

- The object is affectionately cuddled as well as excitedly loved and mutilated.
- It must never change, unless changed by the infant.
- It must survive instinctual loving, and also hating and, if it be a feature, pure aggression.

AFFECT REGULATION

To return to Tyson's question about what promotes the child's capacity to cope with its affects, to regulate itself regardless of whether the mother is directly available or not, it seems to me virtually impossible not to mention the use of the transitional object in this connection. Translated into Winnicottian language, the question could be framed more or less as follows: What are the factors that enable the baby to use the transitional object? I would hazard the answer: to use it as a buffer for its affects of love and hate.

In his clinical and theoretical work, Winnicott develops many versions of the multiplicity of complicated processes of interaction between mother and child, which depend on a facilitating environment and which lead to what Winnicott calls "object-relating"—something I previously termed "having relationship to an object" (Schacht 1973). These are processes that, along the same lines as Winnicott's statement about the transitional object, lead to the object's being "created, not found" (1968a, p. 103). Yet the object must in fact be found in order to be created—a paradox to which Winnicott was the first to draw attention.

In attempting to understand small children who have not succeeded in developing the capacity to use affects in their signal function, Tyson came upon Winnicott's idea of the use of the object. To show where Tyson's arguments and reflections diverge decisively from Winnicott's concept, it will be helpful to recapitulate the principal aspects of that concept. Tyson writes: "Thinking of Winnicott's idea of use of the object, I thought about how unavailable Allen's mother was to him—that it seemed almost as if he had to be emotionally strong to take care of his mother." Tyson goes on to say that while not easy for the mother to hear, this was a turning point; Allen's mother began to use Tyson more constructively, and together they could collaborate on how best to help Allen. Just as, in the case of the use of the transitional object, the entire activity or initiative stems from the subject, which uses the transitional object after it has invested it with life, so, too, it is entirely the subject which is finally able to use the object. The object's sole contribution is that it is there and can be found, and that it survives destruction. The word *contribution* may already be misleading here, since it implies activity. In "Comments on My Paper 'The Use of an Object,' " Winnicott (1968c) mentions the object's task of surviving, and of surviving with the quality of nonretaliation; and he refers, in connection with the destructiveness of the adolescent, to the "containment of what the individual adolescent brings without becoming provoked even under provocation. But this is an application of my new (as I believe) principle of the capacity to use an object arrived at by the subject through the experiences involving survival of the object" (p. 240). And in "The Use of an Object and Relating through Identifications," based on the paper he presented to the New York Psychoanalytic Society on November 12, 1968, Winnicott wrote:

"The assumption is always there, in orthodox theory, that aggression is reactive to the encounter with the reality principle, whereas here it is the destructive drive that creates a quality of externality. This is central in the structure of my argument (1968a, p. 110). Tyson's attribution of the activity or initiative to the object in the following passage seems to me to be based on a misunderstanding: "In other words, the child may have murderous fantasies and erupt in rage, but the mother must reassure the child that his angry, murderous thoughts will not frighten, infuriate, hurt, or kill her." The use of the word *reassure* makes the object responsible for the activity, and the object immediately negates the possibility that the object can be destroyed. Later, Tyson writes that the child can then learn to use the object. She goes on, perhaps again on the basis of a misconception, to say that, once able to use the object, the child can learn from it that there are adaptive ways of gaining control over or handling these emotions.

CONCLUSION

The important point to my mind is that the capacity to use the object results not in learning processes but in the experience that the object lies outside the region of omnipotence, that the object is independent of the ego and not *like* it.

This step is a fundamental one—it is a step outside the realm of the me-only into the world of the me-you.

ACKNOWLEDGMENT

The author thanks Mr. Philip Slotkin, M.A., MITI, for translating her original manuscript from German to English.

REFERENCES

Hartmann, H. (1952). The mutual influences in the development of ego and id. *Psychoanalytic Study of the Child* 7:9–30. New York: International Universities Press.

Kris, E. (1950). Notes on the development and on some current problems of psychoanalytic child psychiatry. *Psychoanalytic Study of the Child* 5:24–46. New York: International Universities Press.

Schacht, L. (1972). Psychoanalytic facilitation into the "subject-uses-subject" phase of maturation. *International Journal of Child Psychotherapy* 1(4):71–88.

_____ (1973). Subjekt gebraucht Subjekt. *Psyche* 27:151–168.

Stern, D. N. (1985). *The Interpersonal World of the Infant*. New York: Basic Books.

Winnicott, D. W. (1951). Transitional objects and transitional phenomena. In *Through Pediatrics to Psychoanalysis*, pp. 229–243. London: Hogarth Press, 1978.

_____ (1968a). The use of an object and relating through identifications. In *Playing and Reality*, pp. 86–94. London: Tavistock, 1971.

_____ (1968b). The use of the word "use." In *Psychoanalytic Explorations*, ed. C. Winnicott, R. Shepherd, and M. Davis, pp. 233–235. London: Karnac, 1989.

_____ (1968c). Comments on my paper "The use of an object." In *Psychoanalytic Explorations*, ed. C. Winnicott, R. Shepherd, and M. Davis, pp. 238–240. London: Karnac, 1989.

6

OBJECT CONSTANCY AND ADULT PSYCHOPATHOLOGY

Salman Akhtar, M.D.

The term *object constancy* was introduced in the psychoanalytic literature by Hartmann (1952) to denote a stage when the growing child's tie to its love object becomes a stable and enduring inner relation independent of need satisfaction. Hartmann viewed this achievement to depend on the development of *object permanence* (Piaget 1937), that is, the cognitive persistence of an object's mental representation in its physical absence, and "a certain degree of neutralization" (Hartmann 1952, p. 15) of the aggressive and libidinal drives. Anna Freud (1965), too, in tracing the development from dependency to self-reliance, spoke of "the stage of object constancy which enables a positive inner image of the object to be maintained, irrespective of either satisfactions or dissatisfactions" (p. 65). The palpable notion that *object* in this context referred mainly to the mother became explicit in Spitz's (1946, 1965) concept of the *libidinal object*, that is, the child's developing an exclusive and stable tie to its mother. It was, however, in the work of Margaret Mahler that the gradual acquisition of object constancy within the context of the mother–child relationship found its most thorough exposition.

In this chapter, I will highlight Mahler's contributions to the concept of object constancy and its attainment during early childhood. I will also discuss the challenges to object constancy posed by subsequent developmental phases, including Oedipus complex, latency, adolescence, young adulthood, and middle age. Following this I will describe various adult psychopathological syndromes associated with failure to achieve object constancy. Finally, I will comment on the implications of these concepts for psychoanalytic process and technique.

THE INITIAL ACHIEVEMENT
OF OBJECT CONSTANCY

Things that always love us, i.e., that constantly satisfy all our needs, we do not notice as such, we simply reckon them as part of our subjective ego; things which are and always have been hostile to us, we simply deny; but to those things which do not yield unconditionally to our desires, which we love because they bring us satisfaction, and hate because they do not submit to us in everything, we attach special mental marks (and) memory-traces with the quality of objectivity. [Ferenczi 1926, p. 371]

Object constancy can be said to have been reached when one particular defense—the splitting of object image—is no longer readily available to the ego. [Mahler and Furer 1968, p. 224]

The predominance of love is the glue of the unified self-representation. [Settlage 1991, p. 352]

Based on extensive observational studies done alone or in collaboration with her colleagues, Mahler (Mahler 1958a,

1958b, Mahler and Furer 1968, Mahler et al. 1975, Mahler and McDevitt 1980) distinguished the psychological birth of the human infant, that is, the beginning in the child of a coherent sense of personhood, from its biological birth. She emphasized that two conditions must be met for organization of the ego and neutralization of drives to arrive at a sense of such personhood: (1) the enteroceptive-proprioceptive stimuli must not be so continual or intense as to prevent structure formation, and (2) the mother must be able to buffer and organize inner and outer stimuli for the infant. Mahler also postulated the sequence of symbiosis and separation-individuation through which the child must pass in order to achieve a fairly stable sense of self and others.

While the "basic core" (Weil 1970) of the infant awakens in a state of enmeshment with the mother's self in the *symbiotic phase*, it is only during the *differentiation subphase* (between 4 to 5 and 8 to 9 months), which is the first subphase of separation-individuation,[1] that the child, inwardly propelled by autonomy strivings, starts to discern his psychic separateness through rudimentary exploration of the self, the mother, and their environment. This is a period of much manual, tactile, and visual exploration of the mother's face and body. There may be engagement in peekaboo games in which the child still plays a passive role (Kleeman 1967). Alongside the seeking of distance from mother is also a greater awareness of her as a special person. This is followed by the *practicing subphase* (between 9 and 16 to 18 months), in which the crawling child, and later the walking toddler, elatedly asserts his new-found psychic autonomy and motoric freedom; buoyed by pervasive secondary narcissism and relatively impervious to external challenges, the child seems involved in a "conquest of

---

[1]Not included in this brief description are the subtle differences in the separation-individuation process of boys and girls (Mahler 1966, 1971, Mahler et al. 1975, McDevitt 1991, Parens 1991).

the world." The elation is, perhaps, also an affective celebration of the escape from engulfment by the mother. Although the child often looks back at the mother for "emotional refueling" (Furer, quoted in Mahler et al 1975, p. 69), his main preoccupation is to exercise his ego apparatuses and widen the orbit of his explorations. This is followed by the *rapprochement subphase* (from about 16 to about 24 months), in which the child senses that his autonomy and psychomotor freedom have their limits and that the external world is more complex than he at first imagined. Narcissistically wounded, the child regresses in the hope of refinding the symbiotic oneness with the mother. The return, however, is an ambivalent one, since the drive of individuation is at work with great force and since the child has become familiar with the ego pleasures of autonomous functioning. This ambivalence has its behavioral counterpart—"ambitendency" (Mahler 1974, p. 161)—insofar as the child poutingly clings to Mother for reassurance, safety, even fusion at one moment, and valiantly distances himself from her for asserting autonomy, control, and separateness the next. If his vacillations are resiliently responded to by the mother and if loving feelings between them predominate over hostile feelings, new regulatory structures begin to emerge (McDevitt 1975). The rapprochement subphase, while turbulent, is also the most significant, since its successful negotiation results in profound intrapsychic alterations, including:

(1) mastery of the cognitively intensified separation anxiety; (2) affirmation of the sense of basic trust; (3) gradual deflation and relinquishment of the sense of omnipotence experienced in the symbiotic dual unity with the mother; (4) gradual compensation for the deflated sense of omnipotence through development of the child's burgeoning ego capacities and sense of autonomy; (5) a firming up of the core sense of self; (6) establishment of a sense of capacity for ego control and modulation of strong libidinal and aggressive urges and affects

(e.g., infantile rage); (7) healing the developmentally normal tendency to maintain the relation with the love object by splitting it into a "good" and a "bad" object, thus also healing the corresponding intrapsychic split; and (8) supplanting the splitting defense with repression as the latter defensive means of curbing unacceptable affects and impulses toward the love object. [Settlage 1977, p. 817]

The last subphase of separation–individuation is termed *on the way to object constancy* (from about 24 to about 36 months) and is associated with self-constancy. This subphase is characterized by the emergence of a more realistic and less shifting view of the self. It is also characterized by the consolidation of a deeper, somewhat ambivalent but more sustained internalized maternal object representation, the libidinal attachment to which does not get seriously compromised by temporary frustrations.[2] The attainment of object constancy assures the mother's lasting presence in the child's mental structure. The attainment of self constancy establishes a coherent, single self-representation with minimal fluctuations under drive pressures. Together these achievements result in (and in a dialectical fashion, are themselves contributed to by) the disposal of aggression toward self and object by repression rather than splitting. Capacity for tolerating ambivalence now emerges on the psychic horizon. The child becomes capable of more complex object relations (Kramer and Akhtar 1988). Inner presence of a "good-enough mother" (Winnicott 1962) diminishes the need for her external presence. Clinging and darting away from her give way to the capacity to maintain "optimal distance" (Bouvet 1958, Mahler 1974), that is, "a

---

[2]Parallel is the development of "reality constancy" (Frosch 1966), which enables the autonomous ego functions "to tolerate alterations and changes in the environment without psychic disruption or adaptational dysfunctions" (p. 350). Kafka (1989) has further elaborated these concepts, interweaving cognition, spatiality, and temporal perspectives in this regard.

psychic position that permits intimacy without loss of autonomy and separateness without painful aloneness" (Akhtar 1992a, p. 30).

The achievement of self- and object constancy is, however, not a once-and-for-all step but an ongoing process. Mahler (1968) and Mahler and Furer (1971, 1974) emphasized that while these descriptions focused on the separation-individuation *phase*, the separation-individuation *process* continues to evolve and stabilize through subsequent development, even during adult life.

SUBSEQUENT REVERBERATIONS

Both achievements—consolidation of individuality and emotional object constancy—are easily challenged by the struggle around toilet training, and by the awareness of the anatomical sexual difference, a blow to the narcissism of the little girl and a danger to the little boy's body integrity. [Mahler et al. 1975, p. 199]

Not until the termination of adolescence do self and object representations acquire stability and firm boundaries, i.e., they become resistant to cathectic shifts. [Blos 1967, p. 163]

Since the subphase *on the way to object constancy* overlaps with the beginning of the phallic-oedipal phase of psychosexual development (Mahler et al. 1975, Parens 1980, 1991), the issues characteristic of it also play a role in the latter. These issues are the replacement of splitting with repression, the emergence of capacity for ambivalence, and the establishment of optimal distance. The oedipal experience requires a unified self with a capacity for intentionality, and objects that are experienced as distinct from oneself and toward whom ambivalence can be tolerated. However, these requirements put the newly acquired self and object constancy to test. Indeed, there exists a reciprocal developmental influence (Parens 1980) between difficulties in separation-individuation and the oedipal phase conflicts. The recently mended split between "good" and "bad" (libidinally and aggressively derived) maternal representations is especially vulnerable to reactivation as the child confronts the contradictory maternal imagos ("madonna" and "whore") of the oedipal phase. Earlier fears of losing the good mother too might resurface in the face of intense castration anxiety. The structuring of object constancy can also be damaged if experiences with the two parents are quite different,[3] as is, to some extent at least, likely during the oedipal phase. The temptations and restrictions of this period also test the capacity for optimal distance. After all, "the task of mastering the oedipal complex is not simply to renounce primary oedipal objects, but to do so in a way that simultaneously permits individual autonomy together with valued traditional continuity" (Poland 1977, p. 410). Moreover, the establishment of incest barrier need not eliminate aim-inhibited subtle affirmations of attractiveness between parents and children. Indeed, there might exist an "oedipally optimal" distance (Akhtar 1992a, p. 35) that is neither incestuously intrusive nor oblivious of cross-generational eroticism, and neither slavishly submissive to early parental injunctions nor totally unmindful of family legacies.

Latency is ushered in by the internalization of parental prohibitions in the form of superego, and characterized by greater cognitive and motor skills. Object constancy is more or less certain. Concerns regarding separation do exist, albeit with a manageable intensity and in amalgamation with sub-

---

[3]Freud's (1923) comment regarding the "conflicts between various identifications into which the ego comes apart" (p. 31) is pertinent here.

terranean oedipal drives. Many games played by latency age
children betray such condensation in displaced, ego syntonic
forms (Glenn 1991).

It is, however, during adolescence that the issues of self-
and object constancy are once again brought to the surface
with full force. This developmental phase, with its characteristic drive upsurge, fosters regression. Adolescents of both
sexes tend to retreat from oedipal conflicts, seeking refuge in
struggles over issues of control, autonomy, and distance.
Regressive tendencies intensify primary self- and object relations. Progressive trends, both defensive and autonomous,
herald new self-configurations and loosening of infantile object ties. On the one hand, renunciation of earlier forms of
object relations paves the way for more age-adequate relationships. On the other hand, regression allows a return to
abandoned ego states, including those involving intense ide-
alizations and devaluations. There is both insistent disengagement from the earlier parental mores internalized in the form
of the superego, and an equally strong reliance on the values of
one's peers and contemporaries. Trial identifications and role
experimentations within the latter context gradually broaden
the ego autonomy and help consolidate a resilient, mature
self-representation. The same is true in the realm of object
representation. In the process of disengagement from primary
love and hate objects, there is a temporary, often intense,
regression to split object relations (Blos 1967, Kramer 1980).
The decathexis of parental object representation is accompanied by heightened narcissism before libidinal investments in
phase-specific, nonincestuous objects become possible. Once
the progressive trends begin to dominate, however, the capacity for object relations deepens in a most meaningful way.
"Indeed, it remains the ultimate task of adolescence to
strengthen post-ambivalent object relations" (Blos 1967, p.
179).

Subsequent life tasks (e.g., separation from parents and

home; engagement and marriage; career choice, often re-quiring the overcoming of ambivalent ties to one's mentors) also revive the vicissitudes of the rapprochement subphase (Escoll 1992). Thus, young adulthood, too, tests self- and object constancy, though to a lesser degree than adolescence. Object constancy can also be strained later by the challenges of raising children. Being the recipient of a child's rapproche-ment subphase turbulence, the mother especially has to mod-ulate her own reciprocal drives and contradictory object representations of the child. Here the maternal object con-stancy comes to serve the "container" (Bion 1967) function for the child's contradictory affects, scattered self-repre-sentations, and vacillating object ties. Subsequently, the capacity to tolerate the child's sexual intrusions, competitive-ness, and hostility during the oedipal phase tests the parental capacity to retain optimal distance. The child's diminished need of parents during latency and the intense, often madden-ing, oscillations in attitudes, affect, and distance during ado-lescence similarly require parental object constancy if all is to go well. Still later, middle age mobilizes a final mourning of the mute and unexpressed self-representations. This is accom-panied by broadening of the core self-representation, and a compensatory deepening of what one indeed has become. Object constancy is also reworked as aggression and envy toward youth, including one's offspring, can no longer be denied, and identifications with one's parents, with all their implicit oedipal ambivalence, are finally buttressed (Kernberg 1980). Finally, during old age, as one approaches death, a deep and postambivalent view of the world that one has lived in and is about to leave needs to be developed in order for this final transition to be smooth.

Having defined object constancy, delineated its initial achievement, and traced its vicissitudes through subsequent development, we are prepared to discuss the adult psychopa-thology associated with its disturbances.

SYNDROMES ASSOCIATED WITH
DISTURBED OBJECT CONSTANCY

The literature abounds in papers and symposia dealing with
the sequalae of the failure of internalization, increased separation anxiety, and other clinical signs that indicate, for example,
the following: that the blending and synthesis of "good" and
"bad" self and object images have not been achieved; that
ego-filtered affects have become inundated by surplus unneutralized aggression; that delusions of omnipotence alternate
with utter dependency and self-denigration; that the body
image has become or remains suffused with unneutralized
id-related erogeneity and aggressive, pent-up body feelings,
and so on. [Mahler 1971, p. 181]

The lack of internalization of the comforting constant mother
is associated with a lack of ego integration. Poor frustration
tolerance and impulse control, fragile self-esteem, and unneutralized aggression leave the patient predisposed to severe
sadomasochistic dispositions and rage reactions. [Blum 1981,
p. 801]

Disturbances of Optimal Distance

The failure to achieve object constancy leads to a continued
propensity to rely excessively on external objects for self-
regulation. Aggression toward them mobilizes fears of having
internally destroyed them, and this, in turn, fuels the need to
closely monitor them in reality. Libidinal attachment and
anaclitic longings, in contrast, stir up fears of enslavement by
external objects, and hence necessitate withdrawal from them.
All this results in a profound difficulty in maintaining optimal
distance. Severe personality disorders constitute a cardinal
example of such psychopathology. Included here are narcissistic, borderline, schizoid, paranoid, hypomanic (Akhtar
1988), infantile, "as-if" (Deutsch 1942), and antisocial per-

sonalities. For them, involvement with others stirs up a characteristic "need–fear dilemma" (Burnham et al. 1969): to be
intimate is to risk engulfment, and to be apart is to court
aloneness. This leads to a variety of compromises. The borderline continues to go back and forth (Akhtar 1990a, Gunderson 1985, Melges and Swartz 1989). The narcissist can
sustain allegiances longer and less frequently shows such
oscillations (Adler 1981, Akhtar 1989, Kernberg 1970). The
paranoid bristles at any change in distance initiated by others
(Akhtar 1990b), preferring the "reliability" of his fear of
being betrayed (Blum 1981). The schizoid opts for withdrawal on the surface while maintaining an intense imaginary
tie to his objects (Akhtar 1987, Fairbairn 1952, Guntrip 1969).
Antisocial and hypomanic individuals, though internally un-
committed, rapidly develop superficial intimacy with others.
This tendency to be highly attuned to others, even magically
identifying with them, is most evident in the "as-if" personalities (Deutsch 1942) and underlies the fraudulent tendency
in all individuals with severe character pathology (Gediman
1985).

Splitting, Emotional Flooding, and Violence

Another result of failed object constancy is the persistence of
split self- and object representations. Splitting gives rise to
repeated, intense, and convincing oscillations of self-esteem
(Akhtar and Byrne 1983, Kernberg 1967, Mahler 1971) that
contribute to an uncertain sense of identity. Such "identity
diffusion" (Akhtar 1984, Erikson 1950, Kernberg 1967) results not only in markedly contradictory character traits but
also in temporal discontinuity in the self-experience; it is a
"life lived in pieces" (Pfieffer 1974). The inner world remains
populated with caricatured part objects. There is incapacity to
understand others in their totality, intolerance of ambivalence, and a tendency to react to realistic setbacks with nega-

tive mood swings (Mahler 1966, 1971, Mahler and Kaplan 1977). In patients with action-prone egos, such flooding with unneutralized aggression might result in destructive and violent acts.

Case 1

Mr. G., a severely borderline young man with an exquisite sensitivity to rejection, was seen three times a week in face-to-face psychoanalytic psychotherapy. Once, early during his treatment, I informed him of an upcoming interruption in the schedule. He responded by pained silence, gaze avoidance, and a noticeable drop in his voice. My empathic affirmation of this and encouragement for him to put his feelings into words met with little success. Later that evening (he told me amid sobs during the next session), Mr. G. saw in his front yard a little frog that appeared sad and lonely to him. He picked up the frog, took it inside, and made a "home" for it in a little box. He tried to cheer up the frog by talking to it and giving it bread crumbs. The frog, however, jumped out of the box and soon was nowhere to be found. Mr. G. looked for it all over his place. He repeatedly called for it, and with the absence of any response began to feel rejected and angry. This grew into rage. Then, suddenly, he saw the frog. Cursing loudly, he chased it around the room, damaging many of his belongings in the process. In a fury, he caught the frog and repeatedly smashed it against the wall with all his might. Later, a dawning awareness that he was "committing murder" stopped him. He let the now badly injured frog out of a window.

The good frog–bad frog split, the shift from caretaker to murderer self, the incapacity for ambivalence, and the flooding of the ego with raw aggression are as explicit in this enactment as are the transference themes of feeling abandoned by me (the bad frog) and consequent loneliness and rage.[4] Blum (1981) notes that in such cases, because of the blurring of self–object boundaries, the object's wish for independence is experienced as an agonizing, hence unforgivable, betrayal.

Paranoia and the Inconstant Object

Less dramatic outcomes are perhaps more common. The distortions of self- and object representations seen in paranoid personality constitute one such instance. The paranoid individual has a close and deep tie with his "inconstant object" (Blum 1981), an ambivalently loved object who appears both needed and persecutory. The inconstant object cannot be allowed to have an independent existence. The issue is not that of closeness with the external object, but intrapsychic separation and the attainment of object constancy. The constant hostile persecution is the reciprocal of libidinal object constancy and "a desperate effort to preserve an illusory constant object while constantly fearing betrayal and loss" (Blum 1981, p. 807).

Inordinate Optimism and the "Someday" Fantasy

In other individuals what appears more prominent is the continued inner clinging to the coenesthetically remembered good mother representation of the symbiotic phase. This may prompt a search for an "all-good" object in external reality. Often this is coupled with a fantasy of "someday" (Akhtar 1991) there being a complete absence of pain and conflict in life. A complex set of psychodynamic mechanisms helps maintain the structural integrity of someday. These include (1) a tenacious denial and negation of sectors of reality that challenge it, (2) splitting-off of those self- and object repre-

---

[4]This case has also been mentioned elsewhere (Volkan and Akhtar 1979).

sentations that mobilize conflict and aggression, (3) a defensively motivated feeling of inauthenticity (Gediman 1985) in those areas of personality where a healthier, more realistic compromise formation level of mentality and functioning has indeed been achieved, and (4) a temporal displacement from past to future of a preoedipal, preverbal state of blissful unity with the "all-good" mother of the symbiotic phase (Mahler et al. 1975). The speculation that this fantasy alludes to a profound longing for a luxurious (and retrospectively idealized) symbiotic phase gains strength from these patients' descriptions of relative inactivity, timelessness, wordlessness, thoughtlessness, unexcited bliss, and the absence of needs in someday. However, other factors, including early parent or sibling loss, intense castration anxiety, and problematic oedipal scenarios, also play a role in the genesis of the someday fantasy.

On an overt level, patients differ in how they strive to reach this someday. Those with a narcissistic personality (Akhtar 1989) actively seek to bring someday to life by hard work and social success. Those with an antisocial bent seek similar magic through swindling, gambling, and get-rich-quick schemes. Paranoid individuals (Akhtar 1990b) focus on the obstacles in their path to someday. Borderline individuals frantically look for someday through infatuations, perverse sexuality, and drugs. Schizoid individuals (Akhtar 1987) adopt a passive stance of waiting for a magical happening, a windfall, or a chance encounter with a charismatic guru. All individuals with a severe personality disorder seem to be seeking a restitution of an inner homeostasis that was disturbed years ago. All are in chronic pursuit.

Malignant Erotic Transference

This pursuit at times gets condensed with positive oedipal strivings. Condensation of the "good" mother representation with that of the desired oedipal partner[5] gives rise to intense longings experienced as unquestionable "needs" (Akhtar 1992b, 1994). During analytic treatment, such powerful erotic transference often turns out to be an upward defense against faulty self- and object constancy. Four aspects of "malignant erotic transference" are especially to be noted: (1) predominance of hostility over love in the seemingly erotic overtures, (2) intense coercion of the analyst to indulge in actual actions, (3) inconsolability in face of the analyst's depriving stance[6], and (4) the absence of erotic counterresonance in the analyst, who experiences such "erotic" demands as intrusive, desperately controlling, and hostile. The choice of the prefix *malignant* to describe such erotic transference is to highlight these features and to extend the context in which this prefix has been earlier used in psychoanalysis, for example, "malignant regression" (Balint 1968), "malignant narcissism" (Kernberg 1989). In such cases, intense narcissism, oral insatiability, and the underlying sadomasochism soon become apparent. These patients cannot reciprocate love and are devouring and consuming with fears of depletion and engulfment. Seeking comfort and contact, they struggle with problems of infantile narcissism, separation, and symbiosis (Blum 1973, p. 69).

Inability to Mourn, Nostalgia, and the "If-Only" Fantasy

The pressure to recapture the preseparation, symbiotic bond impairs the capacity to mourn and underlies the "if-only"

---

[5]The parallel amalgamation of the "bad" mother representation with the oedipal rival creates vengeful hostility which is often split off, denied, or enacted in a contradictory but unassimilated manner, toward the analyst.

[6]Referring to their inconsolability, Freud (1915) termed such patients as "children of nature who refuse to accept the psychical in place of the material" (p. 166).

fantasy (Akhtar 1991). Individuals with this fantasy lack all interest in the future. They constantly wring their hands over something that happened in the past. Focusing their attention on this event, they insist that if only it had not occurred, everything would have turned out all right. Life before that event is retrospectively idealized with a consequent vulnerability to intense nostalgia.[7] The metapsychological structure of the if-only fantasy is similar to that of the someday fantasy. It, too, involves splitting, denial, and primitive idealization. It, too, serves defensive purposes and reflects incomplete mourning over both preoedipal and oedipal traumas. Most frequently, though, the if-only fantasy is a product of incomplete mourning over the loss of the all-good mother of symbiosis. It expresses a position whereby the idealized primary object is neither given up through the work of grieving nor assimilated into the ego through identification.

Case 2

Ms. H., a socially withdrawn, divorced accountant in her mid-forties, was persuaded by her sister to seek help for a rather severe depression of about a year's duration. This was precipitated by her being abruptly left by her married lover of quite some time. Since then, Ms. H. had been in constant agony, pining for him, crying, and contemplating suicide. After some initial stabilizing measures, she began to come for psychotherapy twice a week.

For a long time, our work remained focused on this relationship. Session after anguished session, Ms. H. spoke of this man. They used to meet for a fixed number of intoxicating hours each week. They laughed, played, talked, and made deeply satisfying love. Theirs had been an "ideal relationship," and now she was hopelessly unable to let go of it. Indeed, she

---

[7]Here my views parallel those of Sterba (1940), who saw a longing for mother's breast at the kernel of homesickness, and of Chasseguet-Smirgel (1984), who speaks of the "pervert's nostalgia for primary narcissism" (p. 29).

had held on to everything associated with him: the pillowcase on which he last rested his head, his used napkin, the tissue papers with which he had cleaned himself whenever they made love, his comb, a newspaper he had left in her apartment, and so on. Her place—indeed, her heart—was a shrine and he a god. He was all to her: "mommy, daddy, teddy bear, friend, lover, everything."

As these details unfolded amid heart-wrenching crying, all I could do was to affirm her experience and empathize with her loss. Whenever a discordant note appeared in her descriptions of this man (e.g., his inconsistencies, lying, racial slurs), I underscored it, hoping it would help her de-idealize him and facilitate mourning. Ms. H., however, responded to such interventions with anxiety, hurt, and denial of the significance of his "other side." Soon I saw the premature nature of my interventions and began keeping material regarding his "bad" side to myself.

Over the subsequent months, Ms. H. brought to my office the "linking objects" (Volkan 1981) that connected her with him, often with much emotional flooding. This gradually diminished her preoccupation with him. Still, she was unable to get rid of the things that linked them. Clearly, he had been profoundly important to her. But why? With this, a floodgate opened to themes involving a highly deformed self-image consequent on childhood neglect and abuse.

Ms. H. had been raised by a cold, rule-bound mother and an uninvolved father whose only role was to dole out the violent punishments ordered by his wife. Though affluent, the family bought few things for the children, who often lacked sufficient clothing. Ms. H. had always been called "a monster" and "a disaster" by her mother, who predicted nothing but failure for her life. She had few memories of warmth between them, none of physical closeness. She had grown up afraid that she was bad, even evil. After a forlorn latency and parentally unguided adolescence, Ms. H. entered an out-of-town college. Soon after her graduation, she married a man who turned out to be "a crook and a swindler." Divorced shortly afterward, she underwent a brief period of promiscuity and then settled into a solitary, cynical life. Ten years passed, and then she ran into the older, married man who became her lover.

Significantly, as this information unfolded, Ms. H. only talked of her being bad, ugly, mean, and so on. It had never occurred to her that she had been abused and neglected. Only much later in treatment did she begin to question how her parents had raised her: being sent to a summer camp at age 4, going to get a haircut by herself at age 6, total absence of physical affection (except from a black maid), and repeated beatings by her father. Ms. H. now felt that her "badness" was taking on the blame for how things were and letting her parents off the hook. On the one hand, this realization led to the emergence of violent rage and murderous fantasies toward her parents; on the other hand, it led to an intensified idealization of her departed lover (now also seen by us as a reincarnation of the kind black maid of her childhood).

Significantly, Ms. H. tenaciously avoided the transference allusions of either extreme object representation. She kept me in a neutral though benevolently positive position, sort of like the black maid. Only gradually did it become clear that, having practically no one else in her life, she deeply feared violence from putting me in the "bad" (mother) role and abject dependency from placing me in the "good" (lover) role. We "decided" to continue working in the extratransference realm. Gradually, after some angry confrontations with her parents, Ms. H. began to be more tolerant, though understandably never too kindly, toward them. Her relationship with her sister and brother-in-law now began to deepen, and they slowly came to serve as surrogate parents for her. In this relationship, she became more tolerant of ambivalence. She gradually got rid of the useless items belonging to her lover; she also began jokingly (therefore still partly denying) to talk of his weaknesses and her disappointment in him. As these changes occurred, she developed a fascination for zebras and, at times, laughingly referred to herself as "neither black nor white but striped like a zebra." A restructuring of self- and object constancy was evident.

In sum, lack of object constancy impairs the capacities to mourn, tolerate ambivalence, and maintain optimal distance. Lacking inner cohesion, such individuals tend to develop compensatory structures leading to paranoia, erotomania, and inconsolable nostalgia. These dynamic and structural configurations have considerable bearing on the treatment of such individuals.

TECHNICAL IMPLICATIONS

Rather than recalling, talking about, and reflecting upon the theme, the patient lives out the problem of object constancy with the therapist in the present. For psychotic and borderline patients, object constancy is externally represented by their content in whatever form of ideation, whether of love, politics, films, trash or weather, that serves to maintain the contact with the therapist. Contact between patient and therapist constitutes the agent of both inner and outer negotiation and interaction, out of which emerges the psychological construct of object constancy. [Ekstein and Friedman 1967, p. 362]

Certain configurations persist in transference or acting out patterns which seem to be the outcome of unresolved conflicts in the separation–individuation process. [Mahler 1971, p. 415]

The analytic relationship embodies both therapeutic process and developmental process, and . . . these processes function in a complementary way in the restructuring of object and self constancy. [Settlage 1993, p. 474]

Starting with Loewald (1960) and extending through the later contributions of many analysts (Blum 1971, Burland 1986, Escoll 1977, Fleming 1972, Greenacre 1975, Lax 1986, Schlessinger and Robbins 1983, Settlage 1977, 1991, 1993,

Zetzel 1965), there has evolved a view that the psychoanalytic process has overlaps with the developmental process. A corollary of this position is to see similarities between the analyst–analysand relationship and the mother–child dyad. The technical significance of such a conceptualization depends not only on the analyst's theoretical predilection but also on the analysand's character organization. For the reasonably individuated, neurotic analysand, the analyst's consistent and empathic stance is significant insofar as it permits and safeguards their interpretive undertaking. For the analysand with deficient object constancy, the situation is quite different. The availability of someone empathic, reliable, and constant is a new experience. It stirs up a wide gamut of intense, often contradictory, emotions: disbelief and excitement, anaclitic yearning and anxious withdrawal, hate transferred from early frustrating objects and hope that such hate will not destroy this relationship, and so on.[8] Analysis in such cases remains focused, for a long time, on the anxiety regarding intimacy and separateness, issues of ambivalence, defensive warding-off of aggression, and fears of psychic growth and individuation. Based on my analytic experience with such patients (although, for complex professional reasons, only psychotherapy cases have been reported in this chapter), I have delineated six technical aspects of significance in working with them.

First and foremost, the analyst has to have a greater than usual regard for his "holding" (Winnicott 1960) and "containing" (Bion 1967) functions. Underscoring the role of such noninterpretive ingredients of the analytic technique, Stone (1981) stated that:

---

[8]Manifestations of such affective stirrings are hidden underneath a veneer of oedipal transferences. However, such material is frequently distorted and suspiciously intense. Indeed, "it is often the distortions of the oedipal features that serve as the first clues to unresolved preoedipal issues" (Burland 1986, p. 301).

The "love" implicit in empathy, listening, and trying to understand, in nonseductive devotion to the task, the sense of full acceptance, respect, and sometimes the homely phenomenon of sheer dependable patience, may take their place as equal or nearly equal in importance to sheer interpretive skill. [p. 114]

This is nowhere more true than in the course of treating individuals with disturbed object constancy.

Second, the analyst has to keep in mind that individuals who lack object constancy frequently employ splitting and related defense mechanisms of denial, projective identification, idealization, devaluation, and so forth (Kernberg 1967). Their transferences shift abruptly, and so do their self-estimations. The analyst therefore must retain these contradictory self- and object representations in mind since the patient has a tendency to affectively "forget" one or the other extreme of his experience. The analyst's interpretations, for a long time, might be usefully tempered by his display that he, at least, has not "forgotten" the opposite transference configuration (e.g., "This hate, despite your parallel love, that you feel for me at this time is . . ."). The analyst's allegiance to the "principle of multiple function" (Waelder 1930) also helps reduce his own vulnerability to either/or conceptualizations regarding love and hate, drive and defense, deficit and conflict, the oedipal and the preoedipal, and so forth.

Third, the analyst has to be extraordinarily attentive to matters of "optimal distance" (Akhtar 1992a, Bouvet 1958, Escoll 1992, Mahler et al. 1975). Starting from the time the patient begins to use the couch—or fails to use it (Frank 1992)—through interruptions, vacations, accidental extraanalytic encounters, transference-based oscillations of intimacy, termination-phase advances and regressions, and even afterward, the issue of optimal distance affects analytic technique (Akhtar 1992a). With individuals who lack object constancy, this is only more so. Analysts must be constantly mindful of patients' need for closeness and autonomy and the two corresponding anxieties of fusion and abandonment. Analysts must avoid "interpretative intrusions" (Settlage 1993, p. 24) and often knowingly restrict the expanse of their comments. The first stirrings of longing in a previously detached schizoid patient or a violent enactment in an otherwise agreeable borderline patient, for instance, are better interpreted in the extratransference realm without too quickly unmasking transference allusions. The optimal distance concept also enriches the understanding of "negative therapeutic reactions" (Freud 1923), as these might also arise from separation-based concerns and fears of losing the analyst by getting better (Asch 1977, Grunert 1979, Modell 1965).

Fourth, the analyst has to be sharply attuned to nonverbal communications of the patient. Individuals who lack object constancy more often behave than remember. Their regressive struggle to recapture the symbiotic bond with their mothers defies customary discourse. Fantasy elaboration is meager, and "the raw data pointing to interruptions early in ego development tend to be affectual rather than verbal or intellectual" (Burland 1975, p. 317). The "unrememberable and the unforgettable" (Frank 1969) residues of the preverbal trauma, however, lie unabated under the adult persona and are often discernible only through the patient's posture and movements on the couch, mannerisms, tone of voice, style of entering and leaving the office, and so forth. Paying attention to one's countertransference, where such "behavioral dance and somatic music" (McLaughlin 1992, p. 151) reverberates at its loudest, opens new vistas for reconstruction and insight.

Fifth, the analyst must keep in mind the dialectical relationship between the interpretive resolution of psychopathology and the resumption of arrested development (Settlage 1993). With each undoing of some aspect of pathology, there is the opportunity for resumed development in that area, and with each such developmental advance there is an increase in the patient's tolerance for the exposure of repressed, anxiety-provoking wishes and fantasies. Abrams's (1978) concept of "developmental interpretation" might be a specific tool in this regard. When a hitherto unexpressed healthy tendency emerges as a result of interpretive work, the analyst might underscore the inherent progressive trend and "facilitate the emergence of experiential building-blocks" (p. 397). Settlage's (1993) recent recommendation that the analyst acknowledge and encourage the patient's developmental initiatives and achievements belongs in the same realm.

Finally, the analyst has to recognize that mourninglike elements, integral to all analyses, carry greater significance in the treatment of these patients. This is in part because they have often suffered severe, actual trauma in their childhoods. More importantly, they have not gone through the incremental steps of loss (of external support, of omnipotence) and gain (of internal structure, of reality principle) typical of the separation-individuation process. They lack this prototype of mourning; in Klein's (1940) terms they have not experienced the "depressive position." Separations from the analyst, guilty recognitions of their aggression toward him, dawning gratitude, and the renewed anguish of loss during termination—all awaken and consolidate the process of mourning. The same applies to the loss of their infantile omnipotence and their not infrequent tendency to live in a world of illusions (Burland 1986).

In sum, there are six tasks that seem especially important in analytic work with such patients. These are (1) safeguarding the analyst's "holding" functions; (2) interpreting splitting mechanisms, especially as these pertain to negative transference; (3) maintaining optimal distance; (4) discerning nonverbal communications, especially through countertransference; (5) encouraging developmental initiatives; and (6) facilitating mourning, not only of past losses but also of those inherent in the analytic situation. To balance things out, I will conclude by quoting Blum's (1981) cautionary note about preoedipal reconstructions:

> The transference patterns in cases of very severe developmental arrest and distortions and in cases of severe ego regression do not revive actual infantile relationships in their original form. . . . Analytic reconstruction in these cases is a very complicated effort. Because of projection, denial, splitting, and other infantile defenses, and because of the general invasion of the cognitive process with the primary process, self-object representations are distorted, not only by the patient's specific psychological disturbance, but by the general characteristic of unconscious transformations. [p. 803]

An analytic approach tempered by Blum's wise counsel and yet attending to the six tasks outlined above seems the one best suited for treating individuals with disturbed self- and object constancy.

REFERENCES

Abrams, S. (1978). The teaching and learning of psychoanalytic developmental psychology. *Journal of the American Psychoanalytic Association* 26:387–406.

Adler, G. (1981). The borderline-narcissistic personality disorders continuum. *American Journal of Psychiatry* 138:46–50.

Akhtar, S. (1984). The syndrome of identity diffusion. *American Journal of Psychiatry* 141:1381–1385.

———— (1987). Schizoid personality disorder. *American Journal of Psychotherapy* 41:499–518.

———— (1988). Hypomanic personality disorder. *Integrative Psychiatry* 6:37–52.

———— (1989). Narcissistic personality disorder. *Psychiatric Clinics of North America* 12:505–529.

———— (1990a). Concept of interpersonal distance in borderline personality disorder (letter to editor). *American Journal of Psychiatry* 147:2.

———— (1990b). Paranoid personality disorder. *American Journal of Psychotherapy* 44:5–25.

———— (1991). Three fantasies related to unresolved separation-individuation: a less recognized aspect of severe character pathology. In *Beyond the Symbiotic Orbit: Advances in Separation-Individuation Theory—Essays in Honor of Selma Kramer, M.D.*, ed. S. Akhtar and H. Parens, pp. 261–284. Hillsdale, NJ: Analytic Press.

_____ (1992a). Tethers, orbits, and invisible fences: clinical, developmental, sociocultural, and technical aspects of optimal distance. In *When the Body Speaks: Psychological Meanings in Kinetic Clues*, ed. S. Kramer and S. Akhtar, pp. 21–57. Northvale, NJ: Jason Aronson.

_____ (1992b). *Broken Structures: Severe Personality Disorders and Their Treatment*. Northvale, NJ: Jason Aronson.

_____ (1994). Needs, disruptions, and the return of ego instincts. In *Mahler and Kohut: Perspectives on Development, Psychopathology, and Technique*, ed. S. Kramer and S. Akhtar, pp. 97–115, Northvale, NJ: Jason Aronson.

Akhtar, S., and Byrne, J. P. (1983). The concept of splitting and its clinical relevance. *American Journal of Psychiatry* 140:1013–1016.

Asch, S. (1977). Varieties of negative therapeutic reactions and problems of technique. *Journal of the American Psychoanalytic Association* 24:383–407. New York: International Universities Press.

Balint, M. (1968). *The Basic Fault*. London: Tavistock.

Bion, W. (1967). *Second Thoughts*. New York: Jason Aronson.

Blos, P. (1967). The second individuation process of adolescence. *Psychoanalytic Study of the Child* 22:162–186. New York: International Universities Press.

Blum, H. P. (1971). Transference and structure. In *The Unconscious Today*, ed. M. Kanzer, pp. 177–195. New York: International Universities Press.

_____ (1973). The concept of erotized transference. *Journal of the American Psychoanalytic Association* 21:61–76.

_____ (1977). The prototype of preoedipal reconstruction. *Journal of the American Psychoanalytic Association* 25:757–786.

_____ (1981). Object constancy and paranoid conspiracy. *Journal of the American Psychoanalytic Association* 29:789–813.

Bouvet, M. (1958). Technical variations and the concept of distance. *International Journal of Psycho-Analysis* 39:211–221.

Burland, J. A. (1975). Separation-individuation and reconstruction in psychoanalysis. *International Journal of Psychoanalytic Psychotherapy* 4:303–335.

_____ (1986). Illusion, reality, and fantasy. In *Self and Object Constancy*, ed. R. F. Lax, S. Bach, and J. A. Burland, pp. 291–303. New York: Guilford Press.

Burnham, D. L., Gladstone, A. E., and Gibson, R. W. (1969). *Schizophrenia and the Need–Fear Dilemma*. New York: International Universities Press.

Chasseguet-Smirgel, J. (1984). *Creativity and Perversion*. New York: Norton.

Deutsch, H. (1942). Some forms of emotional disturbance and their relationship to schizophrenia. *Psychoanalytic Quarterly* 11:301–321.

Ekstein, R., and Friedman, S. (1967). Object constancy and psychotic reconstruction. *Psychoanalytic Study of the Child* 22:357–374. New York: International Universities Press.

Erikson, E. H. (1950). *Childhood and Society*. New York: Norton.

Escoll, P. J. (1977). Panel report: the contribution of psychoanalytic developmental concepts to adult analysis. *Journal of the American Psychoanalytic Association* 25:219–234.

_____ (1992). Vicissitudes of optimal distance through the life cycle. In *When the Body Speaks: Psychological Meanings in Kinetic Clues*, ed. S. Kramer and S. Akhtar, pp. 59–87. Northvale, NJ: Jason Aronson.

Fairbairn, W. R. D. (1952). *Psychoanalytic Studies of the Personality*. London: Tavistock.

Ferenczi, S. (1926). The problem of acceptance of unpleasant ideas: advances in knowledge of the sense of reality. In *Further Contributions to the Theory and Technique of Psycho-Analysis*, pp. 366–379. New York: Boni and Liveright, 1927.

Fleming, J. (1972). Early object deprivation and transference phenomena: the working alliance. *Psychoanalytic Quarterly* 21:23–49.

Frank, A. (1969). The unrememberable and the unforgettable: passive primal repression. *Psychoanalytic Study of the Child* 24:48–77. New York: International Universities Press.

———— (1992). A problem with the couch: incapacities and conflicts. In *When the Body Speaks: Psychological Meanings in Kinetic Clues*, ed. S. Kramer and S. Akhtar, pp. 89–112. Northvale, NJ: Jason Aronson.

Freud, A. (1965). *Normality and Pathology in Childhood*. New York: International Universities Press.

Freud, S. (1915). Observations on transference love. *Standard Edition* 12:159–171.

———— (1923). The ego and the id. *Standard Edition* 19:12–68.

Frosch, J. (1966). A note on reality constancy. In *Psychoanalysis—A General Psychology*, ed. R. M. Loewenstein, L. M. Newman, M. Schur, and A. J. Solnit, pp. 349–376. New York: International Universities Press.

Gediman, H. K. (1985). Imposture, inauthenticity, and feeling fraudulent. *Journal of the American Psychoanalytic Association* 33:911–936.

Glenn, J. (1991). Transformations in normal and pathological latency. In *Beyond the Symbiotic Orbit: Advances in Separation-Individuation Theory—Essays in Honor of Selma Kramer, M.D.*, ed. S. Akhtar and H. Parens, pp. 171–187. Hillsdale, NJ: Analytic Press.

Greenacre, P. (1975). On reconstruction. *Journal of the American Psychoanalytic Association* 23:693–712.

Grunert, U. (1979). The negative therapeutic reaction as a reactivation of a disturbed process of separation in the transference. *The Bulletin of European Psychoanalytical Federation* 65:5–19.

Gunderson, J. G. (1985). *Borderline Personality Disorder*. Washington, DC: American Psychiatric Press.

Guntrip, H. (1969). *Schizoid Phenomena, Object Relations, and the Self*. New York: International Universities Press.

Hartmann, H. (1952). Mutual influences in the development of the ego and the id. *Psychoanalytic Study of the Child* 7:9–30. New York: International Universities Press.

Kafka, J. S. (1989). *Multiple Realities in Clinical Practice*. New Haven, CT: Yale University Press.

Kernberg, O. F. (1967). Borderline personality organization. *Journal of the American Psychoanalytic Association* 15:641–685.

———— (1970). Psychoanalytic classification of character pathology. *Journal of the American Psychoanalytic Association* 18:800–822.

———— (1980). *Internal World and External Reality*. New York: Jason Aronson.

———— (1989). The narcissistic personality disorder and the differential diagnosis of antisocial behavior. *Psychiatric Clinics of North America* 12:533–570.

Kleeman, J. A. (1967). The peek-a-boo game. Part 1. Its origins, meanings, and related phenomena in the first year. *Psychoanalytic Study of the Child* 22:239–273. New York: International Universities Press.

Klein, M. (1940). Mourning and its relation to manic-depressive states. In *Love, Guilt, and Reparation and Other Works, 1921–1945*, pp. 344–369. New York: Free Press.

Kramer, S. (1980). Residues of split-object and split-self dichotomies in adolescence. In *Rapprochement: The Critical Subphase of Separation-Individuation*, ed. R. Lax, S. Bach, and J. A. Burland, pp. 417–437. New York: Jason Aronson.

Kramer, S., and Akhtar, S. (1988). The developmental context of internalized preoedipal object relations. *Psychoanalytic Quarterly* 57:547–576.

Lax, R. (1986). Libidinal object and self constancy enhanced by the analytic process. In *Self and Object Constancy*, ed. R. Lax, S. Bach, and J. A. Burland, pp. 271–290. New York: Guilford Press.

Loewald, H. W. (1960). On the therapeutic action of psychoanalysis. *International Journal of Psycho-Analysis* 41:16–33.

Mahler, M. S. (1958a). Autism and symbiosis: two extreme disturbances of identity. *International Journal of Psycho-Analysis* 39:77–83.

_____ (1958b). On two crucial phases of integration of the sense of identity. *Journal of the American Psychoanalytic Association* 6:136–139.

_____ (1966). Notes on the development of basic moods: the depressive affect. In *The Selected Papers of Margaret S. Mahler*, vol. 2, pp. 59–76. New York: Jason Aronson, 1979.

_____ (1971). A study of the separation-individuation process and its possible application to borderline phenomena in the psychoanalytic situation. *Psychoanalytic Study of the Child* 26:403–424. New Haven, CT: Yale University Press.

_____ (1974). Symbiosis and individuation: the psychological birth of the human infant. In *The Selected Papers of Margaret S. Mahler*, vol. 2, pp. 149–165. New York: Jason Aronson, 1979.

Mahler, M. S., and Furer, M. (1968). *On Human Symbiosis and the Vicissitudes of Individuation*. New York: International Universities Press.

Mahler, M. S., and Kaplan, L. (1977). Developmental aspects in the assessment of narcissistic and so-called borderline personalities. In *Borderline Personality Disorders*, ed. P. Hartocollis, pp. 71–86. New York: International Universities Press.

Mahler, M. S., and McDevitt, J. B. (1980). The separation-individuation process and identity formation. In *The Course of Life*, ed. S. I. Greenspan and G. H. Pollack, pp. 395–406. Bethesda, MD: NIMH.

Mahler, M. S., Pine, F., and Bergman, A. (1975). *The Psychological Birth of the Human Infant*. New York: Basic Books.

McDevitt, J. (1975). Separation-individuation and object constancy. *Journal of the American Psychoanalytic Association* 23:713–743.

_____ (1991). Contributions of separation-individuation theory to the understanding of psychopathology during the prelatency years. In *Beyond the Symbiotic Orbit: Advances in Separation-Individuation Theory—Essays in Honor of Selma Kramer, M.D.*, ed. S. Akhtar and H. Parens, pp. 153–170. Hillsdale, NJ: Analytic Press.

McLaughlin, J. T. (1992). Nonverbal behaviors in the analytic situation: the search for meaning in nonverbal cues. In *When the Body Speaks: Psychological Meanings in Kinetic Clues*, ed. S. Kramer and S. Akhtar, pp. 131–162. Northvale, NJ: Jason Aronson.

Melges, F. T., and Swartz, M. S. (1989). Oscillations of attachment in borderline personality disorder. *American Journal of Psychiatry* 146:1115–1120.

Modell, A. (1965). On aspects of the superego's development. *International Journal of Psycho-Analysis* 46:323–331.

Parens, H. (1980). An exploration of the relations of instinctual drives and the symbiosis-separation-individuation process. *Journal of the American Psychoanalytic Association* 28:89–114.

—— (1991). Separation-individuation theory and psychosexual theory. In *Beyond the Symbiotic Orbit: Advances in Separation-Individuation Theory—Essays in Honor of Selma Kramer, M.D.* ed. S. Akhtar and H. Parens, pp. 3–34. Hillsdale, NJ: The Analytic Press.

Pfieffer, E. (1974). Borderline states. *Diseases of the Nervous System* 35:212–219.

Piaget, J. (1937). *The Construction of Reality in the Child.* New York: Basic Books, 1954.

Poland, W. (1977). Pilgrimage: action and tradition in self-analysis. *Journal of the American Psychoanalytic Association* 25:399–416.

Schlessinger, N., and Robbins, F. P. (1983). *A Developmental View of the Psychoanalytic Process.* New York: International Universities Press.

Settlage, C. (1977). The psychoanalytic understanding of narcissistic and borderline personality disorders: advances in developmental theory. *Journal of the American Psychoanalytic Association* 25:805–833.

—— (1991). On the treatment of preoedipal pathology. In *Beyond the Symbiotic Orbit: Advances in Separation-Individuation Theory—Essays in Honor of Selma Kramer, M.D.*, ed. S. Akhtar and H. Parens, pp. 351–367. Hillsdale, NJ: Analytic Press.

—— (1993). Therapeutic process and developmental process in the restructuring of object and self constancy. *Journal of the American Psychoanalytic Association* 41:473–492.

Spitz, R. (1946). The smiling response: a contribution to the ontogenesis of social relations. *Genetic Psychology Monograph* 34:57–125.

—— (1965). *The First Year of Life.* New York: International Universities Press.

Sterba, E. (1940). Homesickness and the mother's breast. *Psychiatric Quarterly* 14:701–707.

Stone, L. (1981). Notes on the noninterpretive elements in the psychoanalytic situation and process. *Journal of the American Psychoanalytic Association* 29:89–118.

Volkan, V. D. (1981). *Linking Objects and Linking Phenomena.* New York: International Universities Press.

Volkan, V. D., and Akhtar, S. (1979). The symptoms of schizophrenia: contributions of the structural theory and object relations theory. In *Integrating Ego Psychology and Object Relations Theory*, pp. 270–285, ed. L. Saretsky, G. D. Goldman, and D. S. Milman. Dubuque, IA: Kendall/Hunt.

Waelder, R. (1930). The principle of multiple function. *Psychoanalytic Quarterly* 5:45–62.

Weil, A. (1970). The basic core. *Psychoanalytic Study of the Child* 25:442–460. New York: International Universities Press.

Winnicott, D. W. (1960). Ego distortion in terms of true and false self. In *The Maturational Processes and the Facilitating Environment*, pp. 140–152. New York: International Universities Press, 1965.

—— (1962). Ego integration in child development. In *The Maturational Processes and the Facilitating Environment*, pp. 56–64. New York: International Universities Press, 1965.

Zetzel, E. (1965). The theory of therapy in relation to a developmental model of the psychic apparatus. *International Journal of Psycho-Analysis* 46:39–52.

7

PROBLEMS IN THE DEVELOPMENTAL CONCEPTUALIZATION OF ADULT PSYCHOPATHOLOGY AND ITS TREATMENT

Discussion of Akhtar's Chapter "Object Constancy and Adult Psychopathology"

Ludwig Haesler, M.D.

In Chapter 6, Salman Akhtar relates the theoretical concept of object constancy to adult psychopathology, and argues that certain clinical phenomena are best understood in terms of some failure in achieving this developmental milestone. Similarly, Akhtar draws parallels and sees "overlaps" between the developmental process and the psychoanalytical process, in which the underlying dynamics of what we understand as psychopathology unfold as specific relational "structures" (Haesler 1991) of transference–countertransference dynamics. Akhtar concludes that there are similarities between the analyst–analysand relationship and the mother–child dyad, and he quotes a number of well-known sources to support his point.

SOME PITFALLS IN CORRELATING ADULT PSYCHOPATHOLOGY AND DEVELOPMENTAL CONCEPTS

Akhtar's approach raises the issue, to which I will return, of what Hartmann termed the *genetic fallacy*, or the danger inherent in attempting to relate what we experience with a patient in a psychoanalytic encounter too directly and crudely to theoretical concepts such as object constancy and, more generally, to our understanding of the whole developmental process. After all, these concepts are the result, as are all our theoretical concepts of human development, of highly generalized abstractions drawn from observation of children, and describe neither the psychic reality of an individual child nor that of the individual adult patient we see in our consulting room. They are generalizations that serve merely to help organize and structure what we observe and experience in ways that allow us to explore and to open up our perception toward a deeper understanding of the unique constellation of intrapsychic conflicts each individual brings and of how he or she relates to the analyst in the psychoanalytic encounter.

When is object constancy fully or sufficiently established? Is it achieved at one specific point in infantile development, or is it more a matter of a gradual development that, as Akhtar shows, continues well throughout the subsequent "phases" of life beyond the separation–individuation process proper at the end of the preoedipal period? And if we consider object constancy to have been fully or sufficiently established, is this a permanent and "fixed" developmental achievement or is it one that may display vacillations at different times in a person's life, in differing inner and outer situations of emotional burden, conflict, and trauma? What technical and overall consequences does "applying" a theoretical concept like object constancy in the manner of medical diagnosis have for the psychoanalytic process? Can we really measure the feelings, expressions, and behavior of the individual patient against a set of concepts based on highly generalized abstractions of observational data, and then rate the clinical phenomena as more or less "pathological," as the result of developmental "failures," or as the expression of a "lack of . . ."? Is this sort of methodological approach useful or detrimental to our clinical work of understanding patients? The two case vignettes Akhtar presents in his paper may help us to answer some of these questions.

SIMILAR DIFFICULTIES VIS-À-VIS THE PSYCHOANALYTIC PROCESS

Discussing the question of possible "overlaps" between the psychoanalytic process and the developmental process, between the analyst–analysand relationship and the mother–child dyad that would justify a technical approach based on the developmental concept of object constancy, we must first keep in mind that the psychoanalytical term *object* refers not to a *thing* bearing specific qualities that may be "objectively" attributed to it but to a complex *relationship*, largely determined by the forces of the dynamic unconscious, in which both participants, subject and object, are involved motivationally and affectively in both conscious and unconscious dimensions. Thus *object* and, accordingly, *object constancy* can be defined and understood only from this relational perspective of the encounter of the analytic couple, that is, from the perspective of the psychoanalytic situation, by carefully reviewing and elaborating an understanding of the complex and highly specific ways, modes, and conditions of this relationship, of its underlying unconscious dynamics, and of the defensive-protective enactment that a patient has acquired and developed in the course of his or her life before entering psychoanalytic treatment.

To view, then, what we call adult psychopathology simply as a regressive revival of a disordered infantile developmental phase that is more or less exactly reenacted as it was then, in the psychoanalytic encounter does not sufficiently take into account that these "pathological" relational structures are the outcome of the elaboration and reelabora-

tion of a wide range of dynamically relevant internal and external factors, of highly complex internal dynamic processes
and the multiplicity of their conditions, of the dynamic transformations of inner and outer experience by drive-ridden
fantasies, wishes, desires, reactions, and so on throughout personality development beyond the separation-individuation
phase proper and in the further developments of later life. So
although what we see and experience with a specific patient,
and the specific relational structures we consciously and unconsciously become involved in and experience as psychoanalysts, may include defensive-protective elaborations and
structures of various kinds, and possibly also aspects of a disordered development of object constancy, we cannot simply
equate the analyst–analysand relationship with the mother–
child dyad and hope to interpret constructively along those
lines.

AKHTAR'S CASES

Mr. G.

The clinical examples Akhtar presents may illustrate my
point. In the first case, that of Mr. G. and the frog, we hear that
the patient was informed by the analyst about an upcoming
interruption in the psychotherapeutic schedule. He responded
with pained silence and gaze avoidance (doing to the analyst
what the analyst had in effect announced he was going to do to
the patient), and a noticeable drop in his voice. Attempts of the
analyst at "empathic affirmation of this and encouragement
for him to put his feelings into words met with little success."
In the next session, Mr. G. reports a terrifying experience
with a frog, displaying his failure in his attempts to find
consolation by enactment and his resulting violent rage.
Akhtar understands the enactment and the violence in light of

the concept of self- and object constancy. Accordingly, the reaction of the patient to the failure is understood as an expression of a "good frog–bad frog split," a "shift from caretaker to murderer self" as an expression of opposing transference themes of feeling abandoned by the analyst (the bad frog), who after his anouncement of the interruption attempts empathically to feed the patient. This interpretation follows the lines of a developmental concept of absence versus presence in a mother–child dyad and its consequences, equating the situation of the patient being abandoned by his analyst with a little longing child going through the experience of not being fed and cared for sufficiently. But does this really help us to understand the dynamics of what happened in the patient and, more important, of the dynamics and development of the transference–countertransference relationship before and after the announcement of the break as it is revealed by the relational structure of this extratransferential experience?

Retrieving the frog from the front yard of his house, the patient tries "to cheer up the frog by talking to it and giving it bread crumbs." The frog, however, does not react to these attempts of the patient in the way the patient expects him to react, but jumps out of its box and is nowhere to be found. After all, we might say, there is no reason to expect a frog to respond either to human talk or the offer of bread. What the patient actually does in his demanding enactment is to project an illusionary idea of cheering someone up by talking to him and feeding him into a frog that, by its very nature, can in no way meet this demand. The patient is caught in a defensive-protective illusion, a defensive narcissification of the object, an attempt to omnipotently control the frog according to his demanding needs, which includes a destructive denial of the reality of the other, of the reality of his *otherness*. In this respect, to see the frog jumping away, not reacting to the expectations of the patient, and to realize its otherness leads to a breakdown of the patient's demand-ridden illusionary denial of reality, liberating all the rage and aggression entailed with this disillusionment until then kept at bay. Accordingly, the bad frog actually is the *frog in reality*, and the good frog a *frog in fantasy*, what Akhtar understands to be a representation of a sort of caretaker self, an object unable to respond to the desire of the patient to reexperience projectively in an active way, under his omnipotent control, what he has failed to find in his encounter with his analyst who, by his actions reveals that he is not the "good" *analyst in fantasy* but an *analyst in reality*, a person in his own right, able to call off sessions.

If these dynamics are really what determines the experience and behavior of the patient, it is understandable that the analyst's efforts to provide "empathic affirmation of this and encouragement for him to put his feelings into words met with little success," as this would only enhance the danger of even more uncontrollable involvement, unless the patient is able curb this danger by reversing roles, by putting himself in the role of the one to enact an interruption of contact, seemingly making the analyst the one who longs for contact by his empathic affirmation.

And from this perspective it seems obvious that the dynamics of the extratransferential experience with the frog and its implications for understanding the transference–countertransference relationship do not simply reflect what the developmental model would refer to as the good and bad, that is, the present, feeding or absent, abandoning mother. They are highly complex defensive–protective elaborations, resulting from active splitting mechanisms in the realm of paranoid-schizoid processes, from denial, projection, projective identification, and omnipotent control over an object. These mechanisms may be "archaic" from a developmental point of view, but they only acquire their character as fixed "pathological" structures in the overall course of development in further life.

Empathic response or, even worse, empathic affirmation alone without interpretation of the underlying dynamics that are always more or less present somehow and somewhere in the actual relationship (e.g., in the frog-patient, breaking off contact with the analyst by pained silence and gaze avoidance) will not succeed in helping the patient out of his destructive, defensive–protective illusion. Rather, the analyst who follows his "technical program" of taking an empathic attitude or of having to be especially empathic with specific patients, and so on, will be trapped by the efforts of such patients, who will eventually instrumentalize the technical program for defensive-protective purposes. And the analyst who follows his technical rules and regulations "correctly" in this way will, because of his systematic "technical" bias, rarely be able to realize sufficiently the problematic character of his actions, how they may affect the actual dynamics, and why in this specific way. Additionally, empathic understanding or empathic affirmation alone will not, in the long run, be able to prevent the destructive breakdown of illusionary defensive narcissification because, sooner or later, the analyst unavoidably will come into play as a person with a reality of his own. The breakdown of this essential form of an illusionary world leads to an experience that, because of the underlying dynamics in these patients, is an essential existential crisis that may trigger overwhelming and uncontrollable destructive rage and violence, as the experience of the patient with the frog demonstrates.

Accordingly, the dynamics of adult psychopathology that may be viewed from the perspective of the concept of object constancy are, as Kernberg shows in his discussions of the fundamental difference between pathological narcissism and narcissism in "normal" infantile development (Kernberg 1975, pp. 270–272), very different from those of normal childhood development. Viewing the psychodynamics of adult psychopathology as they unfold in the analytic encounter simply as expressions of what has taken place in childhood may even be misleading in elaborating the specificity of the underlying dynamics in the here-and-now, the ways reality is conceived, the role of fantasy in extratransferential enactments and their corresponding transferential-countertransferential relational structures or Gestalts, and so on (Haesler 1991), and, especially, the complex ways the analyst becomes involved in these relational Gestalts with his patients in the analytic encounter.

Additionally, equating the psychoanalytical encounter with the patient in the here-and-now with the developmental process, comparing what goes on extra- and intratransferentially to model conceptions based on abstracted generalizations of childhood observation, the analyst runs the risk of losing his psychoanalytical attitude and stance, of becoming more of an analyst who is not so much listening, experiencing, and interpreting what is actually going on in the consulting room as aiming, by comparing the experiential realities he encounters with his theoretical concepts of development, to "diagnose" his patient, pressing her into his specific developmental frame of reference, judging, whether or not the patient has reached this or that stage, whether she is able or not able to do this or that. Subsequently, the analyst becomes someone who judges the patient's developmental "achievements," her assets, abilities, deficiencies, and liabilities, rather than someone who focuses on the experience of the actual encounter, on the patient's and his own personal involvement in it. Consequently, this change from a psychoanalytical to a judgmental "diagnostic" attitude will make him run danger of becoming an analyst who is rather employing specific recommendations and rules of "technique" with patients belonging to specific categories of the diagnostic system of "psychopathological disorders," as Dr. Akhtar is giving them in the last part of his paper, fully in line with this notion, than employing the psychoanalytical method. I shall continue discussing this problem in returning to Dr. Akhtar's second case.

Ms. H.

Akhtar's second case presents a similar problem of a patient engaged in a highly idealized relationship of an extremely illusionary character, including a considerable narcissification of the object, the illusion maintained by the very character of this relationship as one of intense but limited encounters with a man who is married and, accordingly, at her disposal, but only in way that limits the obligations of a more intense relationship that would bind her in a way she would not be able to control sufficiently. She is a divorced woman who has spent most of her life in isolated and socially withdrawn ways, which may already reflect some important aspects of the nature of her inner object relationship. When her lover leaves her, the dynamic function of her illusionary world of an intoxicating "ideal" love relationship threatens to break down, inundating her with uncontrollable destructive rage that she tends to direct against herself in the direction of depressive dynamics, even thoughts of suicide. She succeeds in sustaining her illusionary world, however, preventing the breakdown by trying to continue her highly illusionary relationship by relating to the "things" connected to her experience with the man she made love to. This is a fine illustration of an arrested process of mourning kept at bay by sexualized defensive illusions of an essentially stabilizing character so that "respect for reality" (Freud 1917, p. 244) cannot take the gain.

In her relationship with her analyst she also tends to establish aspects of this form of illusionary relating by "tenaciously avoiding the potential transference allusion," that is, by avoiding seeing the analyst as a different person with a reality of his own who may suggest something significant to think and feel about. Rather, she tries to test his opinions by seducing him to "underscore" discordant notes in her descriptions of this man (e.g., inconsistencies, lying, racial slurs), the analyst hoping that this "would help her de-idealize him and facilitate mourning." And seeing the "premature" nature of his interventions, the analyst begins to keep material regarding the "bad" side of this man to himself, that is, he gives up inquiring about and analyzing, together with the patient, the actual relationship, the specific ways and means of the patient's actions in the here-and-now. Both, in fact, agree (Akhtar writes: "we 'decided' ") to continue working in the extratransferential realm only, giving up working in the realm of transference and resistance and aiming defensively at analyzing only the there-and-then. Thus, the psychoanalytic position of the analyst is finally neutralized and devalued to a "neutral thought benevolently positive position, sort of like the black maid" (a kindly figure from the patient's childhood).

In some cases illusionary denial of the reality of the other may lead, as Akhtar mentions in his paper, to forms of "erotic transference," that is, to highly eroticized forms of relating of the patient, pressing toward the analyst, trying to coerce him to indulge in actual erotic actions as a means of keeping up the illusionary, manipulatively controlled narcissification of the relationship meant to fend off a corresponding destructive potential. Failure to carefully analyze the here-and-now within the realm of the psychoanalytic method may lead to total paralysis in the psychoanalyst, to a destruction of his psychoanalytic function. I have seen several cases of this kind in colleagues seeking supervision because of seemingly insolvable impasses who rationalized abrupt decisions to radically change the whole setting or even to rid themselves of the patients by declaring them unanalyzable or defective or too rigid. Or, when the illusionary paralysis of the analyst's function fails in these cases, when the depriving nature of the reality of the analytic encounter can no longer be kept out of the analytical relationship and denied any further due to chance events, for example, by calling off sessions, taking holiday breaks, or by other events experienced as a disillusionary repudiation, such patients may experience a dramatic breakdown of the illusionary denial of their defensive-protective eroticized transference, which may lead to an explosive release of the destructive potential. Under these circumstances, destructive, self-destructive, or even suicidal acting out may be the outcome of such dynamics not sufficiently addressed by the psychoanalyst.

CONCERNING THE ANALYTIC TECHNIQUE

I wish in closing to comment on the technical recommendations Akhtar makes in the last part of his chapter. He elaborates six major tasks that seem to him to be of importance in psychoanalytic work with such patients, namely, to safeguard the analyst's holding functions, interpreting splitting mechanisms, maintaining optimal distance, discerning nonverbal communications, especially by the use of countertransference, encouraging developmental initiatives, and facilitating mourning, that is, the acceptance of reality, not only of past losses but also of those inherent in the analytic situation. Most of these recommendations with the exception, perhaps, of the more "psychotherapeutic" techniques of actively "encouraging" and "facilitating" refer to well-known aspects of what psychoanalysts do in their work with any of their patients. I cannot see which of our patients would not require what Akhtar points out as specific tasks: safeguarding the analyst's holding function (which is different from simply responding by empathic consolation or affirmation without interpretation); consequent interpretation of splitting mechanisms pertaining to the transference–countertransference relationship;

maintaining an optimal distance; discerning nonverbal communication and carefully using emotional responses. These
tasks refer to the basic principles of the psychoanalytic
method and in this respect I fully agree with Akhtar that
following these tasks will be most effective in helping the
patients he is referring to. This holds as well for psychoanalytical work that is not done in the classical psychoanalytical
setting of four or five sessions per week.

Accordingly, the analyst does not approach her patients
like an engineer employing proper techniques in managing
the problems she encounters with the object of her endeavour,
nor like a surgeon employing the optimal surgical technique
on her patients after having diagnosed the defects, shortcom-
ings, inabilities, and failures she is supposed to correct by
operating on them. Nor does she, like a psychotherapist,
approach patients with a diagnostic attitude, assess the quantity and quality of their disorders, inabilities, deficiencies, and
failures of development in an objectifying way, and then
choose the indication for the adequate and correct technique
for this or that disorder. As a psychoanalyst she seeks rather a
psychoanalytic approach to patients as unique individuals
who use the analyst as object in their own unique ways,
perceived, conceptualized, and interpreted by the analyst
from her specific dual psychoanalytic position as a *participant*
in a unique, largely unconsciously determined relationship,
and, at the same time and also oscillating, as an *observer* of this
relationship, who then communicates her understanding to
patients by means of her tentative, propositional interpretations. These offer patients the opportunity to negotiate freely
their respective responses to these interpretations, finding
"interpretations of the analyst's interpretations" that they
may then again negotiate with the analyst, establishing a true
discourse (Mahony 1987, pp. 69–77) that will open up new
grades of freedom to them (Freud 1923, p. 52). In this regard
the concept of object constancy provides but a very general

frame of reference for understanding adult psychopathology of the kind Akhtar refers to, and is of only limited value in practical clinical psychoanalytic work with these patients.

REFERENCES

Freud, S. (1917). Mourning and melancholia. *Standard Edition* 14:237–258.

_____ (1923). The ego and the id. *Standard Edition* 19:1–66.

Haesler, L. (1991). Relationship between extratransference interpretations and transference interpretations: a clinical study. *International Journal of Psycho-Analysis* 72:463–478.

Kernberg, O. (1975). *Borderline Conditions and Pathological Narcissism*. New York: Jason Aronson.

Mahony, P. (1987). *Psychoanalysis and Discourse*. London: Tavistock.

8

PERSPECTIVES ON INTERNALIZATION, CONSOLIDATION, AND CHANGE

Concluding Reflections

Harold P. Blum, M.D.

The symposium "Development and Disorders of Object Constancy," on which this book is based, elucidated important concepts and themes and posed valuable questions and thoughtful challenges. Object constancy was delineated and refined from a number of different perspectives, various formulations were compared and contrasted, and ideas were tested in the crucible of developmental observations and clinical work.

Object constancy is a key developmental concept with many clinical applications, a landmark in the development of psychoanalytic thought, just as its achievement is a landmark in the development of personality. Unknown during Freud's lifetime, the concept was introduced by Hartmann in 1952 but remained inchoate, with no precise meaning or specific place in developmental sequence and context. The current concept was only gradually formulated by Margaret Mahler and her co-workers. Their work on separation-individuation and object constancy evolved in the approximately fifteen-year period between 1960 and 1975, culminating in "The Psychological Birth of the Human Infant" (Mahler et al. 1975). These very important contributions enriched and stimulated the increasingly complex and sophisticated developmental theory that had begun to evolve after Freud's death and the recovery of psychoanalysis from the ravages of the Second World War and the Holocaust.

Freud had only gradually considered the mother as the primary object of the child's development, as the significance of preoedipal phases and structure formation were accorded more and more prominence. The object was a drive object and was important in the unfolding of the oral, anal, and phallic-oedipal phases. The infant's emergence from primary narcissism presupposed the development of an object relationship. The object participated in development, and there was special emphasis on the role of the object in phase-specific trauma. The infant, for example, might have been orally deprived or anally overstimulated through suppositories or enemas, and the oedipal child might have been threatened with punishment for masturbation or have received direct castration threats. With increasing recognition of the importance of the first object relationship, Freud considered the role of the mother as having central significance. Yet the mother was often presented in relation to her importance in infantile anxiety rather than in the positive facilitation of development. Freud's (1917) concept of a complemental series again involved the interaction of infant and parent, nature and nurture, co-determining and mutually influencing further development.

In Freud's (1926) designation of the great danger situations of childhood, the loss of the object's love referred to the mother–infant relationship. This was a marked shift from consideration of the maternal object primarily as the source of drive gratification or frustration, and prefigured the role of the mother in the development of the infant's sense of security and capacity for self-love and self-esteem. Ego development was emerging from its rudimentary considerations, and when Freud (1923) described the character of the ego in terms of abandoned object cathexes, he was introducing the intertwined importance of ego development and object relations. Ego development was dependent on object relations and identifications, and object relations depended on ego development, including frustration tolerance, anticipation, internalization, the evolution of the reality principle with the sense and testing of reality, and so on. This work was the background for the further development of Hartmann's (1939) important contributions to internalization and its relation to ego development and adaptation: to the work of Spitz, Winnicott, and Anna Freud, and to Mahler's formulation of the process of separation–individuation, and the road to object constancy.

McDEVITT'S CONTRIBUTION

In his elegant elucidation of the concept of object constancy, John McDevitt compares the concepts of different analysts who used the term since Hartmann first introduced it (1952) (see Chapter 2 of this book) in a discussion of a mutual influence of the ego and the id. He recognized that the development of object constancy could be correlated with the child's capacity for relatively independent and autonomous function. Spitz (1959) spoke of the constant libidinal object, noting that a preferential attachment to the mother develops, so that she is a source of pleasure to the infant when she is present and of distress when she is absent. Anna Freud (1965) introduced the concept of the "need-satisfying object." This is really a proto-object and is a prerepresentational formulation. The object is of significance only for the satisfaction of wishes and needs, and the investment in the object or really part object disappears or is withdrawn when the infant is dissatisfied or frustrated. The infant recognizes the source of gratification, for example, much as an infant may cease to cry in anticipation of being fed as it hears its mother's footsteps or the sound of her voice.

It is, indeed, a long way from the need–satisfying object to object constancy, and McDevitt (in this volume) cited Anna Freud's (1965) view that after object constancy has been established, there is a stable relationship to the object that persists whether or not the child is frustrated or disappointed. Mahler (1965), writing at the same time, had already formulated the attainment of object constancy in the third year of life. For Mahler, object constancy meant that the maternal image "has become intrapsychically available to the child in the same way as the actual mother had been libidinally available—for sustenance, comfort, and love" (1968, p. 222). Mahler thus extended the concept of object constancy by giving it a much more complex and significant developmental role. Not only were the timing and sequence for the development of object constancy altered, but object constancy was seen as a gradual process of internalization involving many components. What was important was the development of an internal representation of the mother that was stable, cohesive, and consolidated, uniting all aspects of the mother, libidinal and aggressive, good and bad, within the internal representation. The internal mother may be functionally available and facilitating in a manner quite at variance with the real mother. The infant's specific attachment to the mother, emphasized by Spitz (1965) and A. Freud (1965), should not be confused with issues of person permanence and the capacity to evoke a memory of the absent mother (Fraiberg 1969). And both of these concepts are quite different from Piaget's (1937) concept of object permanence, which deals with the child's capacity to maintain an inner image of an inanimate object after it is hidden. The infant preserves the essential character of the absent physical object in its own time and space. While this is a major cognitive development, closely related to or part of the development of the symbolic process, the inanimate physical object and the living libidinal object have markedly different developmental significance.

Representation of the libidinal object probably begins to develop earlier than that of the inanimate object. On the other hand, object constancy, requiring the integration of loving and hateful aspects of the object relationship and representation, appears to consolidate well after object permanence with respect to the physical object. In Mahler's (1975) conceptualization, summarized here by McDevitt, the conflicts of ambivalence of the rapprochement subphase of separation-individuation must be relatively mastered for the attainment of object constancy. The child's ambitendency will then be relatively overcome, that is, the tendency to cling to and shadow the mother and because of fear of reengulfment to dart away from her and protect the evolving sense of personhood, individuality, and identity. Although the development of object constancy permits the mastery of separation anxiety and the danger situations of loss of the object and the object's love, the crucial issue is not the capacity to tolerate separation but the achievement of intrapsychic separateness. Conflicts are now persistent, for example, the child's wishes and the memories of the mother's disapproving attitudes, her expectations, and prohibitions.

In the case that McDevitt presents, although Donna's rapprochement subphase was more overtly a "rapprochement crisis" than that of most of the other children who were studied, Donna was not able to tolerate angry feelings toward her mother, in part because of the mother's inability to tolerate her own aggression. The mother was overconcerned and overpermissive, transmitting her own fear of aggression to her child. Donna, however, increasingly showed her capacity to function independently of her mother, to derive comfort and affection from the internal object representation. She was free to separate and individuate in other respects and was not subject to abject dependence on her mother, which would have disrupted subsequent development. Donna demonstrated the shift from demanding, clinging relationships to more mature ego development and object relations. The positive affective investment in the object representation indicated that the object was no longer simply a drive object, since the first bonding between mother and infant includes affective exchanges and develops through affectomotor communication along with drive gratification. The affection and affective bonds are consolidated in later development, and we note that Donna at age 2½ was described as warm, empathic, and introspective, with the capacity to care and to form close, meaningful relationships.

In the case of Becky, McDevitt describes a dyad that got off to a bad start. Becky cried frequently, had a sleep disturbance, and was hypersensitive and tense. The emotional unavailability of her mother interfered with basic trust (Erikson 1956). McDevitt makes the important observation that basic trust can be thought of as the inception of the internalization of the representation of the reliable mother as opposed to her actual presence. Becky lacked the elation characteristic of the practicing subphase and developed acute separation anxiety during rapprochement, after her mother withdrew from her emotionally. Instead of consolidating object constancy, the fourth subphase of separation–individuation–heightened ambivalence, marked separation anxiety, and angry and anxious moods continued. She showed conflicts of loyalty and manifested splitting of the object representation. In contrast to Donna, Becky's object representation was ambivalently split and unstable.

Parent–child relationships are variable, and any aspect of the relationship, however distorted through the child's wish-fulfilling and defensive needs, may be internalized. The representations of the object and of the self are not static but are transformed during life so that the nature of the constant object and self, although relatively stable and enduring, may be subject to progressive and regressive transformation. They become vital components of the individual psychic structure.

Disorders of object constancy are not uncommon. Under the threat of conflict or trauma and the resurgence of ambivalence, object and self-representations may be regressively transformed, and object constancy may be impaired. Reassurance against the threatened loss or impairment of object constancy is sought through processes of externalization, identification, and reinternalization of the loving, comforting, and sustaining object.

In adult life, union with a partner is actually an unconscious reunion, reminiscent of Freud's (1925) dictum that the finding of an object is actually a refinding, in this case, of a constant object. This is a culmination of "the road to object constancy." Object constancy is exemplified, affirmed, and required in the marriage vows. For better or worse, in joy and in sorrow, in sickness and in health, in frustration and satisfaction, object constancy is to be established until the irreversible separation of death. Object constancy takes on additional meanings and functions in terms of pledges, values, and ideals. The internal representation of the loving, supporting, approving, and regulating object is a developmental achievement that contributes to the further development of the superego.

THE FOUR COMMENTARIES ON MCDEVITT'S CHAPTER

I shall now turn to the discussion of McDevitt's chapter by Bergman and Meyers of the United States and Berberich and Janssen of Germany.

Anni Bergman

Anni Bergman indicates the significance of identifications in the development of the concept of object constancy and its clinical applications. She underscores McDevitt's thesis that conflict and compromise formation precede the Oedipus complex. Donna, with the help of her optimally available mother, resolved the conflicts of the rapprochement subphase by way of identification with the loving caregiver as well as with the prohibitions imposed by her. Object constancy cannot be achieved without a preceding satisfactory relationship between infant and mother. Lacking this foundation, ambivalent splitting of the object world remains so that the affectionately invested libidinal object does not become a stable intrapsychic representation. It should be noted that this is not defensive splitting of an already integrated intrapsychic representation but a failure of integration due to the lack of predominance of affection over hostility in the mother–infant relationship.

Bergman notes certain parallels between Kleinian theory and the process of separation-individuation elaborated by Mahler. Klein contributed to psychoanalytic developmental theory with her emphasis on the internalization of the good object as a precondition for further developmental achievements. Prior to the depressive position of Kleinian theory, reality is denied and the object is possessed, controlled, and not allowed independence. In Freudian terms, the object would be a narcissistic object incompletely separated, and in Kohut's terms perhaps a selfobject. A major difference lies in the telescoping of development in early Kleinian theory, posing particular difficulty with respect to object representation, object loss, and the mourning process. A mourning process is not possible until the establishment of object constancy with a stable internal object representation, since mourning involves a relative decathexis of the representation of the lost object. In mourning, object loss is acknowledged, but the object representation is not lost. The need for the object is so great in the young child that it is doubtful that a mourning process could occur on the same plane as in the adult or that sufficient ego development has occurred for an effective mourning process. The toddler in the rapprochement subphase does have to come to terms with separateness, loneliness, and relative helplessness, but the experience of loss throughout separation–individuation is offset by the child's gains in ego strength and functional capacities. Furthermore, as McDevitt emphasizes and as Bergman also indicates, the child identifies with the active caregiver on different levels of development. Identification, as Bergman indicates and Blum (1986) noted, is subject to a developmental process. Describing identifications of children with the feeding mother and with the mother who leaves and reunites with the baby, Bergman asks whether early sensorimotor identifications are characteristic for infants who did not receive adequate mothering. Where is the bad mother who left McDevitt's Donna? Donna mothers her dolls while her own mother is out of the room. Was Donna protecting both herself and her mother in her mother's absence? Bergman's trenchant questions cannot be answered without further analytic inferences based on more extensive observational data. Donna may well be protecting herself from sadness and her mother from anger, but Donna clearly does not acutely regress, throw dolls about, or retreat into persistent crying or silent withdrawal. Donna may well be identifying with her mother's reaction formation, but her overall capacity for affectionate play suggests a preponderance of loving over hostile feelings, permitting identification with and internalization of the loved and loving object.

Bergman discusses important issues concerning sexual identification and the development of masculinity and femininity. She appropriately questions McDevitt's statement that the development of boys and girls is the same with respect to

object constancy through the middle of the rapprochement
phase when boys resolve ambivalence and conflict by identifying with their fathers, whereas girls resolve these conflicts
through identification with their mothers. However, from
both observational and clinical points of view, there is great
evidence that boys demonstrate early identifications with
mothers and, similarly, girls with fathers, so that both boys
and girls identify with both parents. While gender identity, a
term that I prefer to sexual identity, is an important component of personal identity and to being an individual separate
from the parent. I am not sure about the value of the concept
of disidentification and have not seen convincing evidence of
such a process.

The earliest identifications are overlaid by later accretions
and transformations. Traces of a boy's preoedipal identification with his mother may usually be observed in analysis,
sometimes including the wish to have babies and to be the
feeding, devouring, engulfing mother, and so on. Boys do
have the problem of moving away from their primary love
objects and primary objects of identification, a factor that may
contribute to their greater proclivity to gender disorder and
problems of sexual identity and perversion. The wish and fear
to be "at one" or merged with Mother, however, and the
threat of symbiotic loss of individuality, the conflicts between
developing individuation and regressive wishes to be and
remain a baby, are problems characteristic of sexes. Otherwise, we would expect to find a preponderance of borderline
cases in women who have not separated from their primary
maternal object and borderline boys with premature pseudo-
independence and reciprocal problems of separation-
individuation. No such sex-linked distribution has been
reported in children or adults with borderline or identity
disorders.

Bergman's discourse on identifications on the way to
object constancy demonstrates the changing nature of identi-

fications from imitative identification to identification with the therapist in the treatment of a severely traumatized child. The identification with the therapist was in the service of attachment, of defense, and of further development. I concur that there is a need for further study of identification and its relation to gender development during separation-individuation. The manner in which parents favor certain lines of development and encourage or discourage specific gender identifications and the parental influence of the child's fantasies, ideals, and values remain important areas for further research.

Helen Meyers

Helen Meyers notes that the establishment of object constancy differentiates the neurotic personality from the more serious forms of psychopathology such as borderline and psychotic disorders. Meyers proceeds to raise and address incisive questions. The constant object representation persists over time, whether the object is present or not, frustrating or disappointing, and so forth. The development of object constancy depends on the interaction with an empathic, attuned, available, safe, and reliable object. Meyers questions whether object constancy depends on a single caregiver or whether it can develop with several caregivers. She suggests that the synthesis of good and bad qualities of the object, the ongoing affective attachment to the good object and its internal representation, and the capacity to evoke and recall this representation in the absence of the external object may occur with several caregivers, but not with too many. Too many caregivers could promote disruptions and confusions of attachment and problems of integration of possibly widely differing relationships.

Is object constancy all or none, or can it fluctuate or fragment? The road to object constancy is long and may be traversed in either direction. Object constancy, Meyers notes, can survive short periods of object loss but may be lost in splitting, fragmentation, and developmental disturbance. Meyers asks whether the establishment of object constancy includes the taming of ambivalence or the tolerance of ambivalence, or are these really the same resolutions of ambivalence? The implication in Meyers's discussion is that the ambivalence really has to be worked through. If the aggressively invested object representation is too strong and the threat to the good object representation is too great, a defensive split may be maintained or integration of the ambivalent love–hate representations may not be achieved. Meyers refers to a capacity to maintain constant objects rather than a specific object relationship, stating that once the capacity is established it does not get lost. I am not sure that object constancy and self-constancy, the capacity for constant object relations, or a cohesive identity can be isolated from the internal representations on which these capacities depend. The internal representations change over time, but there is a continuity in the presence of change. Meyers emphasizes the functional utility of object constancy, for example, coping with separation anxiety in preschool, supporting self-esteem in school, dealing with social and scholastic challenges, contributing to a sense of wholeness in adolescence, and to a dependable, unique identity in adulthood.

Meyers's case of the patient who withdrew and seemed to lose the image of the analyst during separation is of great interest. Like McDevitt's patient Mrs. A., she could not recall the analyst's appearance and, as summer vacation approached, was enraged for weeks. Although regressed to a developmental fixation on the road to object constancy, the analyst and the analysis did not lose all existence for the patient. These cases are extremely valuable for analytic research in areas such as analyzability, capacity for termination, and agents of change. Patients with impaired object constancy test the limits of the analysis and of the analyst. Some such patients may seem to successfully terminate, while others develop severe symptomatic regression with separation panic. A proportion of these patients do not successfully terminate, and the process of returning again and again to the same or different therapists may represent an attempt to negotiate separation-individuation and finally to establish object constancy. Meyers implies that, in addition to interpretation, the constancy of the analytic relationship, and the analyst's dedication, consistency, and reliability, may be important agents of change that permit the gradual establishment of "good-enough" object constancy.

Eva Berberich

In her discussion of McDevitt's paper, Eva Berberich observes that Donna's capacity to tolerate ambivalence is developmentally assisted by her identification with her mother. A caring, comforting, and soothing mother is important to help the child to contain and tame aggression and through identification to be able to engage in self-soothing based on memories of the mother's caring and soothing responsiveness. The attainment of object constancy permits not only tolerance of separation but higher-level object relations, trust, cooperation, and the development of the capacity for concern (Winnicott 1963). Becky, described by McDevitt, had been in analysis since she was 3 years old. Because the relationship between mother and child remained extremely fragile, there was an internal fragility of both the object and self-representation. Unconscious dangers of separation, castration, and death coalesced and were recapitulated in the transference—a transference that was a paramount concern in the life of the patient. I would suggest that McDevitt had also acquired the significance of a new object in the little girl's life. In addition to his role in interpreting transference repetition, the analyst functioned as a lifeline and an alternate object.

Berberich notes that German colleagues use the term *object constancy* more in the sense of constant object relations that are consequent to intrapsychic object constancy and internal separateness. Her case of Lili is most interesting from both clinical and technical viewpoints. The development of object constancy in the child could be observed in relation to a growing integrative and structuring process in the mother. Technically, the conjoint therapy of infant and mother proved to be successful beyond any initial therapeutic optimism. Such application of psychoanalytic knowledge enriched by the understanding of separation-individuation is in its infancy and has much promise for infant psychiatry and the treatment of disturbed mother–infant dyads.

Lili's mother was shocked on first seeing herself reacting as though the infant were someone else's. She was unable to breast-feed Lili, could not enjoy holding her or caring for her, and she felt hate and rage when Lili refused to accede to her wishes. Since the mother tried to open Lili's mouth by force, stuffing food in, in the form of an attack, it was not surprising that Lili developed a feeding problem accompanied by sleep disorders and screaming fits. Lili's mother was horrified at the intensity of her wish to be rid of the child, wanting to forget her, leave her, and give her up for adoption. Lili would cry inconsolably and bite herself when she was angry with her mother. In the very thoughtful and sensitive therapy conducted by Berberich, like the grandmother, the therapist appeared to represent an alternate parent–child relationship, somewhat outside the actual mother–child relationship. Lili could call for help from someone other than her mother, and was perhaps able to deal with the mother and even secure her approval while being protected and supported by the therapist. Berberich proposed that the mother was able to achieve greater maturity within the therapeutic relationship. The therapist was an auxiliary ego and organizing object for the mother as well as for the infant, facilitating developmental and integrative processes in both mother and infant.

Berberich's findings are similar to those of Fraiberg (1969) and Galenson (1991) in the United States. Berberich suggests that the child was able to identify with the mother's maturational process and not simply with the mother's caregiving functions. Identifications with the therapist and also with the grandmother may be presumed. One is reminded of Mahler's comments about infants who can extract mothering; Lili managed to "squeeze blood from a stone." She fought her way to independence from a highly ambivalent relationship that stifled every initiative. Lili's imitation of her mother down to the smallest detail may have represented an identification with the aggressor and a means of winning the mother's affection and approval as a narcissistic object. Subsequently, Lili had further therapy with another therapist, and we learn was asymptomatic during nursery school. While rapprochement issues of separation anxiety, coerciveness, and demandingness remained, it is most gratifying to learn that Lili is active, assertive, and still struggling to attain and maintain object constancy. One is left with many questions, including whether the mother was more adequate in the later subphases of separation–individuation than in the first months of Lili's life, and whether the benevolent effects of later phase reorganization would have a stabilizing effect or would prove to be transitory, especially in the face of later adolescent turmoil.

Paul Janssen

Paul Janssen analytically questions whether there is sufficient evidence to support the notion of object constancy, characterized by the ability to maintain a stable intrapsychic affectionate object representation even when the object is frustrating, disappointing, or absent. Janssen calls for more retrospective studies, utilizing more diverse samples. Perhaps he has in mind the children raised primarily by fathers, by multiple "mothers," or by servants, children of borderline and psychotic mothers, and so forth. Janssen notes that Mahler's ideas have provided an invaluable tool for assessing and treating preoedipal disturbances. Clinical data from patients with borderline personality syndromes, such as "as-if" personalities and addictions, have converged with developmental studies of object constancy and its disturbances. There is a concordance of analytic opinion in many different countries and analytic cultures regarding the lack of integration of ambivalent self- and object representations, primitive object relations, and the absence of a secure sense of identity or self-definition in these disorders.

Because of the primitive infantile nature of these disturbances, somatization and acting out are common. Janssen's group concludes that patients suffering from inflammatory bowel disease somatize their intrapsychic conflicts in this particular pathophysiological system. These patients are subject to disturbances in object constancy, displaying an affective somatization metaphorically expressed as a "scream turned on the body" (Janssen and Wienen 1994). Janssen describes a 21-year-old patient with severe psychological, somatic, and psychosomatic disturbance. She suffered from allergies and had had numerous operations; psychological stress could trigger severe somatization. For example, eczema would erupt after the patient had spoken to or received a letter from her mother. Born prematurely at 8 months, the patient had spent several weeks in an incubator, during which time her mother had nearly died. Janssen posits that the patient became fixated on the instrumental mother, that is, the incubator and medical intervention, but there is also much to suggest an initial disruption of mother–child bonding, attachment, and reciprocity. Therapeutic efforts centered on the patient's relationship with her body and hand contact with the therapist. Did this patient really remain tied to a nonmaternal, inanimate object, or was the patient suffering from a very early preoedipal disturbance? Certainly she sought nurturing and affective resonance as she emerged from her narcissistic withdrawal and extreme somatization.

I would add that allergic patients are very difficult to soothe and comfort and may overtax the mother's ego resources. In such a case (Blum 1991) hypersensitivity led to affective insensitivity and to a cascade of psychological and somatic pathology. Severe itching may tend to interfere with separation-individuation, favoring a narcissistic bodily preoccupation at the expense of object relatedness. The child's overstimulation favors further somatization, a damaged sense of self, and difficulty in integrating painful and pleasurable, loving and hating aspects of the object representation so as to attain object constancy. The dyadic disturbance involves the constitutional allergic hypersensitivity, and the strain this places on many aspects of early development. The child with a severe disorder is both more needy of the object and more frightened of separation, and separation or other threats precipitate and intensify allergic reactions. Janssen's original work, taking into account allergic endowment as well as psychological stress and conflict, extends our notions of the interaction of nature and nurture. Possibly the mapping of the human genome will permit a much deeper understanding of constitutional factors, how they may influence development and parenting, and how their consideration might inform intervention strategies.

TYSON'S CONTRIBUTION

Elaborating on the concept of object constancy, Phyllis Tyson critically compares four different views of its development.

Anna Freud assigned object constancy to the latter half of the second year on the basis of the infant's secure attachment to the mother. Mahler's much more sophisticated idea, however, deals with development of internalized psychic representation and intrapsychic structure formation. Mahler's concept of object constancy, which Tyson notes is now central to analytic developmental theory, requires representational and integrative capacities that are not present until the child has successfully negotiated separation-individuation, usually after the second year of life. Although even a pathological mother–child bond may be maintained as in the abused infant (Solnit and Neubauer 1986), I would prefer to label this type of attachment as enduring rather than constant. The attachment may be suffused with hate, rage, and destructive as well as self-destructive tendencies. The tenacity of the attachment does not describe the quality of attachment, which may sometimes alternate with attack or detachment.

Tyson appropriately draws attention to the development of the child's affective self-regulation, eventually independent of the mother's immediate availability. Self-regulating behaviors emerge within mother–infant exchanges, encouraging identification with the mother's functions as soother, comforter, and regulator, and the development of the infant's own ego functions. The mother's role as auxiliary ego contributes to the child's developing self-regulation. Affect feedback and affect regulation facilitate the development of object constancy, which in turn promotes affect regulation and the emergence of complex affects. Tyson uses Winnicott's (1968) concept of the "use of an object" to elucidate the caregiver's containing, nonretaliatory response to the infant's affect storms. The object to be used is not confused with the subject, and the caregiver must be able to reassure the child that murderous feelings and rageful reactions can be safely survived by both parties. If the caregiver withdraws, abandons, or attacks the infant, then the object cannot be successfully used as an auxiliary ego and holding environment. Various pathogenic interactions appear, which intensify intrapsychic conflict and impede normal development.

Winnicott tended to stress the pathology of the caregiver in the holding environment, but Tyson restores the balance, describing the problems of the hypersensitive and distress-prone infant. The infant may not be able to experience the mother's love and efforts to comfort; the mother's self-confidence and mothering capacities may be undermined by her inability to gratify and soothe the distressed infant and by her lack of pleasurable feedback from her infant. Among the rich and varied clinical illustrations that Tyson offers, the case of Johnny is of particular interest. Johnny had lost at least four caregivers by the age of 3, and his father had not been readily and consistently available. Johnny's resiliency was akin to that of the "invulnerables" (Anthony 1974) who managed to survive and thrive despite psychotic parents and severe, repeated traumatization. These infants apparently have the capacity to use objects as needed, to find alternate objects, and to utilize precocious emerging ego functions. Tyson balances the pioneer analysts' focus on the drive nature of attachment with her emphasis on the role of affect in development from attachment to object constancy.

SCHACHT'S DISCUSSION
OF TYSON'S CHAPTER

Schacht calls attention to the hitherto overlooked historical convergence of the contributions of Heinz Hartmann and D. W. Winnicott in 1951 (though their views were not published until 1952). Hartmann stated, "There is a long way from the object that exists only as it is need-satisfying, to that form of satisfactory object relations that includes object constancy" (1952, p. 163). Schacht then notes the fascinating resemblance of Winnicott's initial concept of the transitional object to Hartmann's introduction of object constancy. Winnicott stated, "But the term transitional object . . . gives room for the process of becoming able to accept difference in similarity . . . a term that describes the infant's journey from the purely subjective to objectivity; and it seems to me that the transitional object (piece of blanket, etc.) is what we see of this journey of progress toward experiencing" (1951, pp. 233–244). Both object constancy and the transitional object are fundamental theoretical and developmental psychoanalytic concepts. Schacht notes their similarity in focusing on the development of object-relatedness. Winnicott and Hartmann both focused on the preoedipal period, but Winnicott on the first differentiation of the "me" and "not-me" and the initiation of separation–individuation. Hartmann's object constancy, as further defined and refined by Mahler, is the culmination of separation–individuation rather than its inception. The transitional object of the middle period of the first year of life coincides with the phase of differentiation, the beginning of the separation–individuation process. Winnicott's contribution complements traditional psychoanalytic theory, which has always emphasized the libidinal investment of the primary object. He believed that the object has the task of surviving the infant's aggression and surviving without being excessively provoked or retaliatory. Winnicott believed that the destructive drive creates a quality of externality, that is, promotes differentiation of self and object. Aggression also contributes to separation–individuation and the development of object constancy.

Winnicott's elucidation of the caregiver's nonretaliatory survival of the infant's aggression is a valuable perspective but limited in its narrow, schematic character. The match between caregiver and infant is very complex, and, as Tyson indicates, the object not only survives but helps to organize the subject. The object provides higher levels of secondary process communication, provides auxiliary assistance in organization and integration, and participates in a continuing dialogue, responding to and changing with the developmental phase of the infant. The object is not only found and created but is, in turn, reciprocally responsive and creative. For the infant to thrive, the object must both survive the infant's aggression and provide affection, protection, stimulation, and dialogue. Affective feedback and communication requires the activity of the object.

Schacht's emphasis on the use of the transitional object to buffer primordial love and hate is a useful perspective, but it appears that the transitional object is not essential for normal development and not all infants have transitional objects. There is some cross-cultural data (Grolnick et al, 1978) suggesting that infants kept in close, direct contact with the parent do not use the transitional object to assist differentiation and the achievement of intrapsychic separateness. The object is there, can be found, and survives destruction. The caregiver survives the infant's destruction with varying degrees of ambivalence and with varying use by the infant of the transitional object, other objects, and so on. The caregiver may regress in the service of the infant's progression, may be drawn into reciprocal regression, or even reverse roles, wanting to be parented by the child.

AKHTAR'S CONTRIBUTION

Salman Akhtar introduces a number of salient clinical and technical perspectives. Dealing primarily with failures and disorders of object constancy, he describes a wide variety of syndromes that may occur. A failure to achieve object constancy and a state of object inconstancy may be associated with paranoia and with erotomania. A malignant erotic transference may defend against a persecutory and hateful transference. There may be nostalgic wishing for the good symbiotic mother, excessive clinging to idealized fantasy objects, evident, for example, in dependence on charismatic persons, support groups, drugs, and so on. Intimacy risks engulfment and enslavement, and separation courts object loss and identity diffusion. Akhtar shows that there can be a variety of compromises and oscillations between withdrawing and clinging, shadowing and darting away, a hypomanic search for a union with the object and antisocial assaults on the bad object. The "as-if" personality has not achieved object or self-constancy and may undergo chameleon-like changes in relation to different objects. Many borderline personalities demonstrate the need–fear dilemma, being frightened of both attachment and loss. In severe promiscuity there is a desperate need for a narcissistic object with whom there can be bodily contact, while attachment is avoided and the inevitably bad object is aggressively discarded. Akhtar's consideration of excessive optimism may be balanced with consideration of extreme pessimism, with expectations of inconsolable disappointment, both in the self and the object.

Akhtar provides examples of severe adult psychopathology, emphasizing the likelihood of an underlying disturbance in object constancy. Drawn from psychotherapy cases, probably because such severe pathology would militate against engagement in a psychoanalytic process, his data are persuasive, though not so compelling as would have been possible with psychoanalytic cases. In Akhtar's first case, the patient had a profoundly regressive reaction to being informed of an upcoming interruption in schedule. Attributing human qualities to a frog, he attempted to cheer and comfort it, talking to it and feeding it. The frog at this point presumably represented the patient who felt abandoned by the analyst. When the frog jumped away, however, and seemingly rejected the patient, the analyst was the frog-man; feeling rejected by the frog as he felt rejected and abandoned by the analyst, the patient attempted to smash the frog in a murderous rage. Akhtar infers the blurring of self–object boundaries in the rage over the inability to control the analyst, with the threat of loss of ego organization and impulse control concomitant with loss of the good organizing object. These inferences are consistent with Akhtar's review and utilization of separation-individuation theory for the understanding of the patient's severe psychopathology.

HAESLER'S DISCUSSION OF AKHTAR'S CHAPTER

Haesler questions both the theoretical premises and the technical precepts that Akhtar espouses. I will focus on two of the important points that Haesler elaborates. Haesler points out that it is inaccurate to view the later manifestations of psychopathology and the reverberations of object constancy from the oedipal phase to old age and up to death without taking into account developmental complexity and the differences in psychic structure and function between early childhood and adult life. Parallel to this issue, Haesler questions to what extent the analytic process may be considered to be a developmental process and to what degree observational data may inform analytic data. Haesler is critical of the notion of the transference–countertransference relationship simply mirroring the analysand's early preoedipal developmental process, as if the transference reproduced the original infantile disturbance of separation-individuation.

Haesler indicates that the possibility of a genetic fallacy must always be considered in preoedipal genetic interpretations and reconstructions. Aware of problems regarding literal transference repetition, Akhtar concludes his paper citing this author's caveat, "transference patterns in cases of very severe developmental arrest and distortions and in cases of severe regression do not revive actual infantile relationships in their original form" (Blum 1981, p. 803). Even when we speak of how infantile certain borderline patients and other severely ill patients are in many areas of the personality, the implied comparison does not concretely mean that the adult patient is an infant.

In his discussion, Akhtar points to the preoedipal influence on the Oedipus complex and how, for example, the contradictory images of the madonna and whore of the oedipal phase may be superimposed on a split from the preoedipal period that was never fully healed. The reelaboration of adolescence in adult life to which Haesler refers is undoubtedly the outcome of internal and external factors that Akhtar does not choose to stress in his singular focus on object constancy. The adult psychopathologies are, indeed, more than a regressive revival of infantile developmental disorder and necessarily have important elements and features of later life. In the same sense, the adult neurosis is not simply a reactivation of the infantile neurosis, but is in many ways a later edition and modified derivative of the infantile neurosis. As previously indicated, I am not sure if the later editions of object constancy are best described under that rubric. As object constancy evolves, it seems to me that both its representations and functions are in many ways absorbed by the superego as well as self-soothing and self-sustaining ego functions.

Haesler refers to the "extratransference sphere" regarding both of Akhtar's illustrations. Haesler has also written on extratransference and has stressed that the same constellation of unconscious intrapsychic conflicts may be found inside and outside the transference. Akhtar's first case, however, may exemplify the classical acting out of the transference, the relationship with the frog representing the analytic dyad. This is quite different from the analyst representing the patient's father while interpreting that the patient simultaneously lives out a dependent, maternal relationship with his wife. Though extratransference interpretations may be very important and sometimes the most immediately significant locus of clarification and interpretation, Haesler appropriately stresses the need for careful analysis of the analytic relationship. A focus on life outside, or on the past, may be used to defend against the transference and vice versa. While the transference is not an end in itself, no patient will understand himself or herself, including infantile attitudes, fixations, conflicts, traumas, and character disturbance, without the analysis of the transference to its genetic roots.

Akhtar's technical recommendations, as Haesler notes, are indeed applicable to most patients. Not all patients, however, are as in need of support, analytic tolerance, and patience as are very ill patients, nor are they as sensitive to issues of tact and timing. For the very ill patient, the experience of analysis as a holding and facilitating environment may be essential to the capacity to assimilate interpretation and insight. These patients are not comfortable either with intimacy or with separateness and separation. They may oscillate between the two or choose one particular defensive mode such as withdrawal. There is no optimal distance because of the unresolved preoedipal developmental disturbance that has contributed to the intensity and lack of resolution of later unconscious conflicts. Perhaps it might be useful to think of "optimal distance" as the flexible capacity for both separation and intimacy. This capacity is related to tolerance of the separation-in-intimacy of the analytic situation.

CONCLUDING REMARKS

The analytic situation is the crucible and testing ground for both the clinical application of theory and for drawing theoretical inferences from clinical work. The discussions are relevant to the contemporary controversies of conflict versus deficit, experience versus insight, the here-and-now of the transference versus genetic reconstruction. Some polarization is useful for heuristic purposes and is simultaneously reminiscent of issues of splitting versus integration. Object constancy is a concept that is in the process of theoretical integration and clinical application. Object constancy, the fourth phase of separation–individuation, was not meant to substitute for crucial considerations of unconscious conflict. Object constancy is a sophisticated conceptual contribution to psychic structure and function. It has contributed to understanding of normal development and of psychopathology. The disorders of object constancy do not call for changes in analytic technique, but point to a greater awareness of the subtleties of the analytic process and the conditions that may call for genetic interpretation or modified analysis or for rationally based psychoanalytic psychotherapy. Object constancy is a necessary precondition for mourning, self-constancy, and reality constancy (Frosch 1966). At the same time, our concepts are not constant, and advances in our knowledge of development and disorder will doubtless lead to changes in our developmental and theoretical concepts.

REFERENCES

Anthony, E. J. (1974). The syndrome of the psychologically invulnerable child. In *The Child and His Family*, vol 3, ed. E. J. Anthony and C. Koupernik. New York: John Wiley and Sons.

Blum, H. P. (1981). Object inconstancy and paranoid conspiracy. *Journal of the American Psychoanalytic Association* 29:789–813.

——— (1986). On identification and its vicissitudes. *International Journal of Psycho-Analysis* 67:267–276.

——— (1991). Hypersensitivity and insensitivity: allergic disposition and developmental disturbance. In *The Course of Life*, vol. 3, ed. S. Greenspan and D. Pollock. New York: International Universities Press.

Erikson, E. (1956). The problem of ego identity. In *Identity and the Life Cycle*, pp. 104–164. New York: International Universities Press, 1959.

Fraiberg, S. (1969). Libidinal object constancy and mental representation. *Psychoanalytic Study of the Child* 24:9–47. New York: International Universities Press.

Freud, A. (1965). *Normality and Pathology in Childhood*. New York: International Universities Press.

Freud, S. (1917). Mourning and melancholia. *Standard Edition* 14:237–258.

_____ (1923). The ego and the id. *Standard Edition* 19:3–66.

_____ (1925). Negation. *Standard Edition* 19:235–239.

_____ (1926). Inhibitions, symptoms, and anxiety. *Standard Edition* 20:75–174.

Frosch, J. (1966). A note on reality constancy. In *Psychoanalysis—A General Psychology*, ed. R. M. Loewenstein et al., pp. 349–376. New York: International Universities Press.

Galenson, E. (1991). Treatment of psychological disorders of early childhood: a tripartite therapeutic model. In *Beyond the Symbiotic Orbit: Advances in Separation-Individuation Theory—Essays in Honor of Selma Kramer, M.D.*, ed. S. Akhtar and M. Parens, pp. 323–336. Hillsdale, NJ: The Analytic Press.

Grolnick, S. A., Barkin, L., Muensterberger, W. (eds). (1978). *Between Reality and Fantasy: Transitional Objects and Phenomena*. New York: Jason Aronson.

Hartmann, H. (1939). *Ego Psychology and the Problem of Adaptation*. New York: International Universities Press.

_____ (1952). The mutual influences in the development of the ego and the id. In *Essays on Ego Psychology*, pp. 155–182. New York: International Universities Press, 1964.

Janssen, P. L., and Wienen, G. (in press). Group analysis with ulcerative colitis and regional ileitis: The discovery of the scream. *Group Analysis*.

Mahler, M. S. (1965). On the significance of the normal separation-individuation phase. In *Drives, Affects, Behavior*, vol. 11, ed. M. Schur, pp. 161–169. New York: International Universities Press.

_____ (1975). On the current status of the infantile neurosis. In *The Selected Papers of Margaret S. Mahler*, vol. 2, *Separation-Individuation*, pp. 189–194. New York: Jason Aronson, 1979.

Mahler, M. S., and Furer, M. (1968). *On Human Symbiosis and the Vicissitudes of Individuation*, vol 1, *Infantile Psychosis*, p. 222. New York: International Universities Press.

Mahler, M. S., Pine, F., and Bergman, A. (1975). *The Psychological Birth of the Human Infant*. New York: Basic Books.

Piaget, J. (1937). *The Child's Construction of Reality*, trans. M. Cook. London: Kegan Paul, 1955.

Solnit, A. J., and Neubauer, P. B. (1986). Object constancy and early triadic relationships. *Journal of the American Academy of Child Psychiatry* 25:23–29.

Spitz, R. A. (1959). *A Genetic Field Theory of Ego Formation: Its Implications for Pathology*. New York: International Universities Press.

_____ (1965). *The First Year of Life*. New York: International Universities Press.

Winnicott, D. W. (1951). Transitional objects and transitional phenomena: A study of the first not-me possession. In *Collected Papers: Through Paediatrics to Psychoanalysis*, pp. 229–242. London: Tavistock, 1958.

_____ (1963). The development of the capacity for concern. In *The Maturational Processes and the Facilitating Environment*, pp. 73–82. New York: International Universities Press.

_____ (1968). The use of an object and relating through identifications. In *Playing and Reality*, pp. 86–94. London: Tavistock, 1971.

Index